PRINCIPLES & CHOICES

Book Two

TRUTH AND REASON

by Camille Pauley and Robert J. Spitzer, S.J., Ph.D.

Nihil Obstat: Very Rev. David Mulholland, J.D.
July 30, 2012

Imprimatur: Most Reverend J. Peter Sartain
Archbishop of Seattle
Given at Seattle, Washington
on August 17, 2012

A significant portion of the content in this text
is based on the following two books, and is used
with permission of the copyright holders:

• *Ten Universal Principles: A Brief Philosophy of
the Life Issues,* by Robert J. Spitzer, S.J., Ph.D.
(San Francisco: Ignatius Press, 2011).

• *Healing the Culture: A Commonsense Philosophy
of Happiness, Freedom, and the Life Issues,* by
Robert J. Spitzer, S.J, Ph.D. (San Francisco:
Ignatius Press, 2000).

Scripture passages are from the Catholic
Edition of the Revised Standard Version of the
Bible, copyright 1965, 1966 by the Division of
Christian Education of the National Council
of the Churches of Christ in the United States
of America. Used with permission. All rights
reserved.

Thank You!

The authors wish to express their profound gratitude to the following individuals and organizations who made significant contributions to this work:

Michael Pauley – Copy Editor

Carron R. Silva, M.A.T. – Curriculum Design Specialist and Teaching Coach

Lynn Kittridge – Curriculum Design Specialist and Classroom Beta-Test Lead

Mark Shea – Scripture and CCC Annotations

Sheila Cowley – Graphic Design and Layout

Professional Support – Lisa-Ann Oliver, Kaelen Burton, Erika Rudzis, Monica Burrill, and Michael Friedline

Student Support – Jeffrey D'Angelo, Toni Fuller, Bayli A. Hochstein, Alyssa Kubinski, Aaron Manry, Peter Montine, Tori Moran, Maria E. Rillera, Ashlene Silva

Grateful acknowledgement is also given to the many individuals and organizations who made this work possible, including: Camille and Dale Peterson, M.J. Murdock Charitable Trust, AJ and Jody Mullally, Richard and Julie Thrasher, Holy Family Catholic Church – Kirkland, WA, John Buehler, Richard and Nancy Alvord, Robert and Annmarie Kelly, Fraser Family Foundation, Robert and Elizabeth Crnkovich, Richard and Maude Ferry, Richard and Patricia Miailovich, Alex and Stephanie Sheng, Dominic Parmantier, Bernie and Joyce Kaifer, Gellert and Elizabeth Dornay, Michelle Dotsch and Jay Hoag, Doris and James Cassan, Michael and Mary Bernard, Richard and Jill Black, John and Angela Connelly, Robert and Pam Gunderson, Stephen and Shannon Murphy, Susan Rutherford, Frederic and Martha Weiss, John and Donna Lugar, Michael and Judy Kostov.

Special thanks to the students and religion teachers at Eastside Catholic High School in Sammamish, Washington and McGill-Toolen High School in Mobile, Alabama, for serving as the beta-test sites for our pilot study.

About the Authors

Camille Pauley is the creator and principal author of the *Principles and Choices*© high school curriculum. She is also the author of the *Robert and Emma* series—a play in four acts. Camille is president and co-founder of Healing the Culture, which educates people on the unique dignity of human life; and founder of Being With, which trains individuals to provide compassionate visitation to people with debilitating or terminal illnesses or injuries. Camille has spoken to thousands of audiences, has co-produced six video series, and has been an influential voice on television, radio, and print media. She holds an M.A. in Communication from Washington State University. She and her family live in Seattle, Washington.

Robert J. Spitzer, S.J., Ph.D., is the author of the books upon which the *Principles and Choices*© curriculum is based, including *Healing the Culture* and *Ten Universal Principles*. He is co-founder of Healing the Culture, and former President of Gonzaga University. Fr. Spitzer has inspired millions of people with his books, video series, television programs, and lectures on everything from the dignity of the human person to proofs for the existence of God. He holds a Ph.D. in Philosophy from Catholic University of America. Fr. Spitzer is founder and President of the Magis Institute for Faith and Reason in Irvine, California, through which you can purchase the popular high school curriculum: *The Reason Series: What Science Has to Say About God.*

Contents

Chapter One: Truth. **1**

    What is Truth?. 2

    Two Kinds of Truth 3

    Relativism 4

    Self-Evident Truth. 5

    Evidence of Truth in the Physical World 5

    Factual Truth. 7

    Is Reality Just an Illusion? 7

    If There is Scientific Truth,
        is There Also Ethical Truth? 9

    Common Understanding 10

    Reason 10

    Conscience 12

    Divine Revelation. 15

    Conclusion. 15

Chapter Two: Principles of Reason **17**

        Ten Universal Principles of Civilization 18

    Principles and Definitions 19

        The Principle of Non-Contradiction 21

        The Principle of Complete Explanation. 23

        The Principle of Objective Evidence. 24

    Conclusion. 25

Chapter Three: Defining the Human Person **27**

    How to Define Something 28

    Four Steps to Uncovering a Real Definition
        (A "Complete Explanation"). 30

    Testing Our Theory on an Acorn. 31

        Physical Description. 31

        Powers 31

        Conditions 31

        Full Purpose 32

        The Definition 33

    Defining a Human Person. .33

        Physical Description. 34

        Powers 34

        Conditions 36

        Full Purpose 36

        The Definition 37

    Your Choice. 38

Chapter Four: Application to Social Issues. **39**

    Abortion and the Principle
    of Non-Contradiction 42

    Abortion and the Principle
    of Complete Explanation 44

    Abortion and the Principle
    of Objective Evidence. 49

    Conclusion. 51

Appendix. **52**

Glossary. **53**

Endnotes **54**

Index **55**

Check it out!

Enter the codes you'll find in your textbook here...

www.principlesandchoices.com

Like us on Facebook and share your thoughts...

www.facebook.com/principlesandchoices

Follow our tweets for up-to-date news and views...

twitter.com/prinandchoice

Check out videos from our team and friends around the world...

www.youtube.com/user/principlesandchoices

PRINCIPLES & CHOICES

Book Two

TRUTH AND REASON

WHAT IS LIFE ALL ABOUT?
HOW DO WE FIND TRUE HAPPINESS?

IF YOU HAVE TRIED TO FIND ANSWERS TO QUESTIONS LIKE THESE, YOU HAVE BEEN ENGAGING IN PHILOSOPHY.

© Sabphoto / Fotolia

CHAPTER 1: Truth

CHAPTER ONE
KEY TERMS

common understanding

conscience

ethical relativism

ethics

deadened conscience

factual truth

first principles

morality

objective ethics

objective truth

philosophy

reason

relativism

revelation

self-evident truth

subjective truth

truth

Have you ever spent time thinking about the really important things in life — like what life is all about, whether there is a God, whether people have free will, and how to find true happiness? Have you wondered why suffering happens, what is good and evil, and where you will go after you die?

If you have ever tried to find answers to questions like these, you have been engaging in **philosophy**.

Aristotle was a philosopher who lived in Greece more than 2,400 years ago. He is considered one of the most influential philosophers the world has ever known. Aristotle defined philosophy as "the knowledge of being" — or the study of what is **true** about reality versus what is **not true.**

The word "philosophy" literally means, "love of wisdom" — from the Greek words **philo** (meaning "love") and **sophia** (meaning "wisdom"). Good philosophers love to discover what is true so that they can become wise.

What Is Truth?

Errol Morris is an Academy Award-winning filmmaker who produced a documentary called, "The Thin Blue Line." The film is about an innocent man named Randall Adams who was wrongly convicted of murder and sentenced to die. Because of the documentary, the actual murder case was reopened. It was discovered that Randall Adams was innocent, and he was set free.

Was Mr. Adams truly guilty when people thought that he was guilty, and then he suddenly became innocent when people later realized that he was innocent? Or is it really the case that what people *thought* didn't matter — he was either guilty or innocent as a matter of *fact*, and could not be both?

Addressing this question, the filmmaker told the story of a bet he had with a friend when he was 10 years old. His friend believed that Los Angeles was west of Reno, Nevada. Errol Morris claimed that it wasn't. They bet two dollars, and Errol pulled out a map. Sure enough, Los Angeles was actually *east* of Reno, Nevada; so his friend claimed that the map was wrong, and Errol never got his two dollars.

While recounting this story on a radio program, Mr. Morris said:

> *There is such a thing as truth, but we often have a vested interest in ignoring it or outright denying it. Also, it's not just thinking something that makes it true. Truth is not relative. It's not subjective. It may be elusive or hidden. People may wish to disregard it. But there is such a thing as truth and the pursuit of truth.* **A**

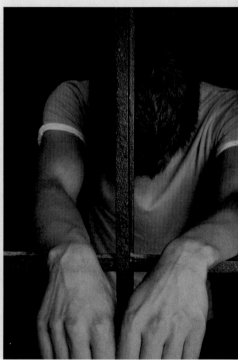

© andreykr / Fotolia

Aristotle defined truth in the following way: "To say of what *is* that it *is not,* or of what *is not* that it *is,* is false; while to say of what *is* that it *is,* and of what *is not* that it *is not,* is true." **B**

In other words, if an apple is red, but you say, "That apple is NOT red," then your statement is false. If your brother does NOT like mayonnaise, but you say, "My brother likes mayonnaise," then that statement is also false.

On the other hand, if the sky is blue, and you say, "The sky is blue," then your statement is true. And if a square is NOT round, and you say, "That square is NOT round," then that statement is also true.

Whatever corresponds with what is real, is true. Whatever does not correspond with what is real, is false. Studying what is true and what is false is the foundation of both science and philosophy.

TWO KINDS OF TRUTH

From the above examples, you may have noticed that there are two different kinds of truth. They are called "subjective truth" and "objective truth."

Subjective truth means a state of reality that can change depending on who is perceiving it, or where or when it is being perceived. For example, the statement, "mayonnaise tastes good," is a subjective statement because it depends on a number of factors, including who is doing the tasting, what brand of mayonnaise is being tasted, and whether the mayonnaise is being tasted before or after the expiration date.

Objective truth means a state of reality that is either self-evident or that people can verify by using their five senses (factual truth). Objective truth does not depend on anyone's opinions. It is not affected by the personal feelings or biases of the people observing it.

> **Self-evident** = true by definition; contains its own evidence or proof, and doesn't need further demonstration.

For example, the statement "squares can never be circles" is objectively true because it is **self-evident**. In geometry, the very definition of a square requires that it have four inscribed right angles. Circles, by definition, have no right angles. So it doesn't matter who is looking at the square, where they are, what month it is, or even how good the person's vision is. Self-evident objective truths are true for all times, places, and persons. The fact that squares can never be circles is true today, it was true one hundred years ago, and it will still be true one hundred years from now. It is true whether you live in the northern hemisphere of the earth, or the southern hemisphere, or on the Moon. It is true no matter who you are — whether you are rich or poor, young or old, famous or obscure, intelligent or illiterate. Self-evident objective truth is "universally true." We find these truths most often in mathematics, logic, and metaphysics — which is a branch of philosophy dealing with God, infinity, and other ultimate realities.

> **SELF-EVIDENT OBJECTIVE TRUTHS ARE TRUE FOR ALL TIMES, PLACES, AND PERSONS.**

The second kind of objective truth is **factual truth.** These are truths which can be verified through the senses of sight, hearing, smell, taste, and/or touch. For example, if you are holding a cup in front of the classroom, everyone with the sense of sight and a reasonable degree of sanity will agree that it is factually true that you are indeed standing in front of the classroom, holding a cup.

All science is grounded in this kind of objective truth. As you probably know, science begins with observable data — either data that we ourselves can observe, or data that we observe by measuring it with instruments.

But factual truth is not universal in the same way that self-evident truth is. Remember in our example of a "square not being a circle," we observed that the characteristics of a square today are the same as they were a hundred years ago, and they'll still be the same a hundred years in the future. But with factual truth, the evidence you can observe with your five senses may change frequently. You may be holding a cup in front of the classroom, but then you set it on the floor. You may be reading a specific temperature on a thermometer, but a moment later it has changed. So we say that factual truth must be linked to a specific place and a specific time. We can say, for example, that the weather is sunny today and the temperature is 75 degrees. That statement may be objectively true where you live, and at the time you observe it. But a town 500 miles away may have different weather. And even in your town, the weather and temperature might be completely different an hour later.

> **IF THERE IS NO TRUTH, THEN YOU CANNOT CLAIM IT TO BE TRUE THAT THERE IS NO TRUTH.**

RELATIVISM

We sometimes hear people arguing that there is no such thing as truth, or that all truth is relative. This belief is called **relativism**.

For example, Bethany tells us that she is a "relativist." She claims that there is no such thing as objective truth, and says, "Truth is a changing mixture of what I experience, what I think and believe, the opinions I have formed, the feelings I have on a particular day, the environment in which I grew up, and the culture in which I live. Truth is different for every person, and can even change within a person from time to time."

There are two logical fallacies with a relativist position. First, if Bethany claims that there is no such thing as objective truth, then she doesn't have any way to defend her own position. If there is <u>no truth</u>, then she cannot claim it to be <u>true</u> that there is <u>no truth</u>. It's like saying, "The objective fact is that there are no objective facts." The statement is incoherent, because it contradicts itself.

Secondly, Bethany's claim contradicts real experience, as we have seen with the examples of factual truths and self-evident truths discussed earlier. The next section will further explain this.

Pi (π) is the 16th letter of the Greek alphabet, and in mathematics the letter is used to symbolize the circumference of a circle divided by its diameter. This number is tremendously important, especially for people who work in professions that use physics. Engineers rely on this number to determine the arcs in the structures they are building.

When you divide the circumference of a circle by its diameter, you will always get 3.14159265358979323846... The ellipses (...) indicate that the number goes on forever. No matter what size circle you have, *pi* will always equal 3.14159265358979323846...

Unfortunately, this is a very inconvenient number. Imagine how difficult it would be to work with this number if you lived during a time when there were no computers and no calculators.

During such a time, in 1897, an amateur mathematical hobbyist by the name of Dr. Edwin J. Goodwin convinced Indiana state legislator Taylor I. Record to submit a bill that would have rounded off *pi* to the nice and easy—but wrong— number 3.2. The bill actually passed the Indiana State House of Representatives by a vote of 67-0.

On the day that the bill was read to the Senate, a mathematics professor by the name of Clarence Abiathar Waldo happened to be visiting the State Capitol on other business, and learned of the bill. He informed the senators of the catastrophes that would occur if the state of Indiana arbitrarily changed the value of the number. Fortunately, the bill died before becoming law.

If an engineer were to substitute the number 3.2 for *pi*, any building using this new number would be structurally compromised and would likely collapse. Any bridge would not meet in the middle. Any wheel would have a bump in its rim.

Think about what might have happened if Professor Waldo had not believed in objective truth and had not convinced the legislators that his opinion was better than Dr. Goodman's. There are real consequences to disregarding objective truth.

EVIDENCE OF TRUTH IN THE PHYSICAL WORLD

There is truth in the physical world. You can hold an opinion about what is true and what is false, but all opinions about the physical world are *not* equal. Some opinions are true and some are false. Some are more true than others. Some explain more than others (they are more "complete"). Some apply in more situations than other opinions (they are more "universally applicable").

Take, for example, what happened in the field of physics between 1905 and 1927. Before 1905, people thought that Sir Isaac Newton's principles of physics were correct. Indeed, some of them were correct, and still are; but some of his theories were later proved incorrect. For example, Newton thought that the universe had an infinite amount of space, time, and mass; and he thought that space in the universe corresponded to Euclidian geometrical principles. Because of that, he believed that the shortest distance between two points is always a straight line. But, as the great physicist Albert Einstein showed later on,

© Claudiad / iStockphoto

Sir Isaac Newton was quite wrong about these opinions.

How did the world of science come to believe that Einstein's opinion was right, and Newton's opinion was wrong? Because Einstein's opinion was based on a *more complete set of data*. In the time that passed between Newton and Einstein, more scientific instruments were invented, more research was carried out, and new information was discovered. Armed with more information, Einstein was able to show the errors in Newton's thinking, and put forth a better theory.

We will discuss this further in the next chapter on principles of reason, but in the end, Einstein's opinion was more *complete* than Newton's opinion, and so we judge Einstein's opinion to be better, that is, truer than Newton's.

EINSTEIN'S EXPLANATION WAS MORE COMPLETE THAN NEWTON'S EXPLANATION, AND SO EINSTEIN'S OPINION WAS BETTER.

Now, if a student were to say in class, "I like Newton's opinion better," the teacher would probably ask, "Why? Einstein's explanation is more logical and more complete." If the student answered, "I don't know… Just because," then the teacher could say, "That's unreasonable and irresponsible." And she would be right.

In your academic, personal, and professional life, you will want to hold opinions that are the most logical, explain the most, and apply to the most situations. Why? Because, as we shall see, these are the best opinions. People who don't care whether their opinion is true or not usually find it very difficult to succeed in school, work, and personal relationships. This attitude can have serious consequences. Consider the fictional story in the next section which illustrates this point.

FACTUAL TRUTH

Let's say Robert is a relativist who does not believe in objective truth. His science teacher, Mrs. Tan, is a chemist. One day, Mrs. Tan is working on an experiment in class, and she gets a headache. She cannot leave her potentially explosive experiment, so she asks Robert to grab some aspirin from her chemical cabinet in the back of the room.

Upon opening the cabinet, Robert discovers dozens of unmarked bottles filled with pills. He selects a bottle whose contents appear to resemble aspirin. He takes out two pills, puts them in his hand, and looks at them. They look like aspirin. They feel like aspirin. Robert becomes strongly convinced that they are aspirin. So he brings them to Mrs. Tan with a glass of water, and she swallows them.

Now let's say, for the sake of the argument, that what Robert gave to Mrs. Tan was not aspirin, but cyanide. What will happen? Remember, Robert is a relativist.

Obviously, the fact that Robert believes truth is just a matter of opinion doesn't make a bit of difference to the cyanide tablets. Mrs. Tan will certainly die all the same.

It does not matter that the pills look and feel like aspirin. It does not matter that Robert **believes** the pills are aspirin. It does not even matter that his intentions are good. The presence of cyanide in the pills is an objective fact, independent of Robert's perceptions. And it is absolutely true that consuming cyanide is incompatible with human life.

IS REALITY JUST AN ILLUSION?

What about the argument that all reality is ultimately just an illusion? Somebody might say, "How can you prove that there are really other people in this room?" or "How can I truly know that everything I am seeing and experiencing right now isn't just part of a dream?"

IS THIS THE REAL WORLD OR AN ALTERNATE REALITY? HOW DO WE KNOW?

This idea has generated some interesting science fiction stories, but it just doesn't add up. The fact that nearly all people of reasonable intelligence can affirm the existence of other people in the room reveals the likelihood that those other people are *really* there. It is highly improbable that two or more people could have exactly the same dream experience within their own completely separate and individual thought worlds.

So then someone might argue, "Well, maybe our minds are all controlled by some supercomputer which is forcing us all to perceive ourselves in the same dream, interacting with each other, when we're really not."

Again, that's an interesting thought, but it does not seem to be a reasonable or responsible belief about the nature of the real world. Aristotle showed 2,400 years ago that all human knowledge is based on certain "first principles" which are necessary to accept before you can prove or

 Use code **PCS211** to read Aristotle's thoughts on this.

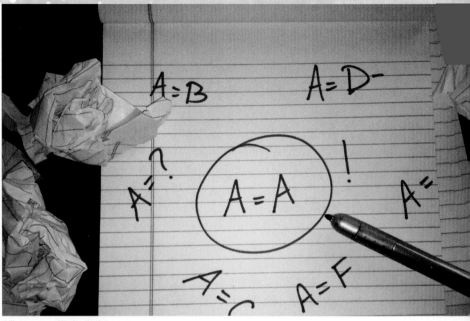

© Photo courtesy of Healing the Culture

disprove **anything**. First principles are so basic that they do not need to be proved by other proofs. They prove themselves.

For example "A = A" is a first principle. You do not need to prove that A = A. The equation is true because it proves itself. Aristotle argued that it was reasonable to believe in the truth of these first principles because they are self-evident, and had shown themselves to be reliable in countless circumstances. He noted that it was also responsible to believe in them because denying them would put an end to human thinking!

FIRST PRINCIPLES ARE SELF-EVIDENT. THEY PROVE THEMSELVES.

You can also see how human progress would be halted if we couldn't agree on these first principles. If people cannot accept that "A=A," then it is impossible to see how they could accept more complex descriptions of reality, such as the law of gravity or laws of medicine.

Following this principle, it is reasonable and responsible to believe that you are you, and you really exist, and so do all the other people in the room, and that we are not all in a dream world having the same dream. It's necessary to accept this as a "first principle" before you can prove or disprove anything else. To deny it would make it impossible for us to carry on any intelligent conversation or debate any issue ever again.

IF THERE IS SCIENTIFIC TRUTH, IS THERE ALSO ETHICAL TRUTH?

The following three chapters in this book will focus on objective truth in the physical world. We will make use of three logical principles (or "principles of reason") to produce an objective definition of the human person. Once we do that, we will be able to use our objective definition to evaluate difficult questions, such as whether an unborn child is a unique and individual human person or just a "blob of cells" or a "potential person." The answer, of course, has significant consequences in the abortion debate.

But you may have heard the argument that while there is objective truth in science, there is no objective truth in morality or ethics. **Morality** refers to the good or evil nature of human actions. **Ethics** refers to a set of standards by which a community judges the rightness or wrongness of human actions.

The argument goes like this: because we can see, taste, touch, smell, and hear physical things, those things are real, and we can know what is true about them. We can see gorillas and monkeys with our eyes, so we know that they are real.

But since we cannot see good or evil by looking through a microscope, and we can't feel right or wrong with our hands, or taste them with our tongues, "good" and "evil" are not real. "Right" and "wrong" are matters of opinion, custom, tradition, and belief, and they can change depending on the situation.

Therefore, what one person calls "right" or "wrong" is just an opinion. We cannot make any *universal* statements about right or wrong, good or bad. Any thought about what is good or evil may be true for one person but not for another. It may be true for one culture, but not for another. It may be true at one time, but not at another. This belief is called **ethical relativism** (sometimes called "moral relativism" or "situation ethics"). This hypothesis holds that there are no real objective standards for determining right or wrong conduct.

Standing in opposition to this view is the argument that there *is* such a thing as objective moral truth, and it exists for everybody, in every place, and in every time. This position argues that there are objective standards for judging human acts.

Objective ethics holds that goodness is an actual reality that exists in itself. It is not just a theory or a principle, but a real, existing entity. Christianity and certain other world religions hold that the reality of goodness is God Himself. Therefore, God is the absolute standard by which we can determine what is good and what is evil.

There are several ways that we can know there is objective moral truth, and objective standards of ethics. They include common understanding, our ability to reason, conscience, and divine revelation. Let's briefly look at each of them.

THE SILVER RULE

Baha'i: *Ascribe not to any soul that which thou wouldst not have ascribed to thee.* [C]

Buddhism: *Hurt not others in ways that you yourself would find hurtful.* [D]

Christianity: *Judge not, that you be not judged.* [E]

Confucianism: *Never impose on others what you would not choose for yourself.* [F]

Hinduism: *One should never do that to another which one regards as injurious to one's own self.* [G]

Islam: *What you dislike to be done to you, don't do to them.* [H]

Judaism: *That which is hateful to you, do not do to your fellow.* [I]

COMMON UNDERSTANDING

The phrase "common understanding" means "thinking that is shared in common with most other people." When **most** reasonable people in **most** places in **most** ages of history share the same understanding about what is good and what is evil, there is a strong probability that what is being understood is true.

Obviously, people in various places and times have believed things to be good which are actually cruel or even evil — such as cannibalism and slavery. But there have always been people who objected to these practices, and ultimately the vast majority of people have come to understand that these things are cruel and evil.

With rare exceptions, it has been the common understanding of humankind that murdering innocent people is wrong. Nearly every civilization that has ever existed has had laws or rules against murder. And most of them have also had laws or rules against stealing, cheating, and lying. The fact that there are occasionally terrible exceptions to this moral consensus should not blind us to the reality that, in fact, a consensus can be discerned throughout the course of history.

Furthermore, many major religions have, in one form or another, an ethical law that is often referred to as the "Silver Rule" ("Do **not** do unto others what you would **not** have them do unto you"). The side box on this page contains some examples.

These common rules point strongly to the existence of objective ethical truth which is accessible to people in every nation and in every generation.

However, even large groups of people over long periods of time can be misled and confused. For thousands of years, many people thought slavery was acceptable. Did that make it right? If there is objective ethical truth, we need more than just a study of history to prove it.

REASON

Reason is the ability of the human mind to think about things logically. By using our reason, we can see that certain ethical rules are necessary for our very existence.

For example, we can use reason to conclude that all human beings need life. Without life, we would not even be able to have this discussion. Therefore, a rule prohibiting murder makes rational sense.

But we also need community. Human beings are social creatures, and we rely on relationships within a society of people to find meaning and fulfillment. When people are left in solitary confinement for long periods of time, they often become psychologically, emotionally, spiritually, and even physically ill.

Of course, there are healthy communities and unhealthy communities. Healthy communities build up persons, uphold truth and justice, and direct human relationships toward

> MANY PEOPLE THOUGHT SLAVERY WAS ACCEPTABLE. DID THAT MAKE IT RIGHT?

© wildpixel / iStockphoto

Use reason to show that slavery is wrong. Start with the idea of freedom. Why is freedom necessary for human beings to be fully human? How does slavery harm human relationships and the health of communities? Write your thoughts below.

faith, hope, and love. Governmental authorities, churches, schools, and families are healthy when they exist for this purpose. Unhealthy communities oppress persons, violate principles of truth and justice, and steer relationships toward distrust, cynicism, and selfishness.

Using reason, we can conclude that anything which threatens the life of a person or the health of a community is objectively wrong.

So, for example, murder is wrong because it destroys human life, which is necessary for our existence. Drug and alcohol abuse is wrong because it harms human health and threatens human life. It also damages community by impairing good judgment in our actions toward others.

Lying, cheating, and stealing are wrong because they destroy the trust which is necessary for human relationships to thrive. Without trust, communities and societies collapse.

We can also use reason to conclude that anything which harms our relationship with God is wrong. For example, we can determine that cursing God is wrong because it harms our relationship with Him.

Using the intellect's capacity for reason is a second way to arrive at truth. It makes sense that killing people is contrary to the nature of human beings. It makes sense that lying and stealing will break down relationships and destroy communities. It makes sense that cursing God undermines our relationship with Him.

However, when we are in particular situations, faced with a choice of acting one way or another, there is a third way to discern objective ethical truth. It is related to reason and is called "conscience."

CONSCIENCE

Conscience is the ability of your reason to judge, here and now, whether a particular act you have done, or are doing, or are about to do, is good or evil.

Think back to a time when you felt very troubled before performing a particular act, and very guilty after carrying it out. What was it about that act that troubled you and then brought on the guilty feelings?

We seem to have a built-in sense of when an act is evil. This sense causes us to be troubled or even repulsed. If we go through with the act, it is as if we have taken the evil of that action into ourselves and it causes us to feel alienated from ourselves (not at home with ourselves). We say we feel "guilty."

It's almost as if we have a sixth sense not only to perceive evil, but to feel its negative presence. When we cooperate with evil, we feel its negativity inside of us.

But our conscience isn't limited to revealing only those actions that are evil. It also tells us about actions that are good.

When we do something good, our consciences cause us to feel good, honorable, or noble. When we do something wrong, our consciences cause us to feel bad, guilty, or ashamed. It is the conscience which, deep inside, makes us want to do what is right and avoid what is evil.

> ## "HUMAN BEINGS, ALL OVER THE EARTH, HAVE THIS CURIOUS IDEA THAT THEY OUGHT TO BEHAVE IN A CERTAIN WAY, AND CAN'T REALLY GET RID OF IT."
>
> —*renowned Christian author, C.S. Lewis*

Every day we are faced with choices to do what is right or what is wrong. Think about the last time you had the choice to tell the truth or tell a lie. Try to think about a more serious situation, rather than a time that you were just kidding around and having fun. Maybe you were being asked by your parents or someone else about whether you had done something that you didn't want to admit.

If you chose to tell the truth, did you have a sense deep in your heart that you did the right thing? It may have been difficult to tell the truth, and it may have meant getting into trouble or being embarrassed. But deep inside, did you feel right about being honest? If so, your conscience was responding to your choice.

But what if you chose to lie? Did it make you feel bad that you did not tell the truth? Maybe you felt relief about not getting into trouble, but deep inside did you feel guilty that you had deceived someone who cared about you? Did you have a sense that you did wrong by lying? If so, that was your conscience speaking to you.

Now, if there were no such thing as acts that were truly good, and acts that were truly bad, then where does our conscience come from? What is causing it to respond? And why do all of our consciences so often respond in the same way toward the same kinds of acts?

Some people argue that our consciences are just signs that we have been brainwashed or conditioned into feeling noble or guilty about particular acts. But is this really possible for everyone? Is it realistic to suggest that all of humanity from the beginning of time has been brainwashed or conditioned to feel proud of good acts and ashamed of bad acts? If you survey thousands of years of history and literature, the human capacity to feel guilt or shame over committing evil or harmful acts is seen as a universal human characteristic.

Besides, can you really brainwash a person into learning how to feel troubled, alienated, and repulsed by something? Unless you already have the capacity to feel these things in the first place, no amount of brainwashing will cause you to feel them. If you stand in front of a monkey and lecture him sternly about stealing your banana, he might feel fear or amusement, but he does not appear to be feeling repulsed or alienated at the evil of his action. He may be sad to have disappointed you, but he does not appear to be in a state of guilt — tossing and turning at night because he feels that his action was intrinsically wrong or unjust.

Now some actions can cause either a negative or positive feeling in our conscience immediately. For example, if an average person (not a sociopath) were to kill someone unjustly, or ruin someone's reputation by lying about her, or cause great injury to his best friend by driving drunk, his conscience would probably react immediately with guilt, regret, and long-lasting anxiety.

However, there are other actions where the evil is not as immediately apparent to our consciences. For example, it might not be apparent to some students that plagiarism is wrong until a teacher explains to them that stealing someone's ideas is just as wrong as stealing someone's things. Certain kinds of lies may seem harmless until someone explains how it damages our integrity in the minds of others, and even in our thoughts about ourselves. Many little children don't think it's wrong to grab a few pieces of candy from a big display in a grocery store. Someone has to explain to them that it is unjust, and that if everyone did it, the merchant would go out of business.

Consciences can be wrong through ignorance. For example, Harold finds ten dollars on the counter and is unsure whether it belongs to him or to his sister. He shrugs his shoulders and pockets the money. If the money belongs to his sister, Harold would be guilty of stealing. It doesn't matter that he didn't know for sure who the ten dollars belonged to. Harold *knew* that he didn't know. We are responsible if we deliberately fail to take reasonable steps to educate ourselves about what is true.

But a person's ignorance might occur through no fault of her own. If a person *does* try to learn what is true, but then unintentionally does something wrong, we would not accuse that person of being evil or bad.

When a parent, teacher, pastor, or other person explains why certain less

© ktaylorg / iStockphoto

As you look for truth in the world, you may find it helpful to use the four tools in this chapter: **common understanding, reason, conscience, and divine revelation.** There are many false messengers, and many deceivers. Can you call to mind some of these false messengers as you think about things you have seen in the media, Hollywood, the music and fashion industry, advertising, and other areas of culture?

© Sabphoto / Fotolia

obvious actions are wrong, this input helps form our consciences. It gives our consciences additional information about when to feel troubled and when to feel noble. When our minds work together with our consciences, then we have the best possibility of making good decisions and avoiding evil ones; of building up society rather than destroying it; of helping people rather than damaging them. A well-formed conscience helps us to be a positive influence in the world rather than a negative one.

Sometimes a person has committed a wrong act for so long that she no longer hears the voice deep inside, telling her that it is wrong. This is called a "deadened conscience."

Psychologists have found that some people who have committed terrible crimes have stifled their consciences

WHO FORMED OUR ANCESTORS' CONSCIENCES? ...AND THEIR ANCESTORS BEFORE THEM?

by a lifetime of acting against it. Such criminals will frequently say, "It no longer seemed wrong." For a conscience to work, it must be followed.

The key point here is that human beings have a responsibility to learn right from wrong. We have a responsibility to form our consciences properly.

How are people's consciences ordinarily formed? Normally by parents, teachers, and religious figures. But who formed *their* consciences? The answer is — an earlier generation of parents, teachers, and religious figures. So does the whole process keep on going forever? As a matter of fact, it does not. If we look back into history, most of the principles that have been used to help form our consciences have come from religion — or what might be called **divine revelation**.

DIVINE REVELATION

Human beings need God to reveal right and wrong to us. Without God, we eventually fall into confusion, disagreement, and division. In the Bible, Saint Paul warns us of this in the letter to the Hebrews:

Jesus Christ is the same yesterday, today, and forever. Do not be led away by diverse and strange teachings.
(1 Hebrews 13:8-9)

The Bible helps steer us toward what is true and guides us in how to live our lives. It is filled with clear instructions about what is good and what is evil. For example, in Matthew 19, Jesus reveals the validity of the Ten Commandments, and says:

You shall not kill, you shall not commit adultery, you shall not steal, you shall not bear false witness, honor your father and mother, and you shall love your neighbor as yourself.
(Matthew 19:18-19)

As you can see, Jesus did not stop at the Ten Commandments. He adds, "love your neighbor as yourself." And then He goes further and declares that the entire law and prophets are summed up in the commandment to love. When He does this, He makes love higher than all the commandments, and shows that what makes the other commandments valid is that they support love:

You shall love the Lord your God with all your heart, and with all your soul, and with all your mind.' This is the great and first commandment. And a second is like it, 'You shall love your neighbor as yourself.' On these two commandments depend all the law and the prophets.
(Matthew 22:37-40)

CONCLUSION

Truth is real. Its existence is real, regardless of what we think. Therefore, our thoughts about what is true can be right, but they can also be wrong.

This is true not only in the world of physics, but also in the world of ethics. There are objective physical truths and objective ethical truths, and when we disregard them, there are unhappy consequences.

In the remainder of this book, we will focus on physical truth to answer the question: "Is the fetus a human person?" Chapter 2 will lay out three principles of reason. Then in Chapter 3, we will use these principles to formulate an objective definition of human personhood. That definition will help us to evaluate the difficult moral issue of abortion in Chapter 4.

Use code **PCS212** to access vocabulary and other study tools for this chapter.

CHAPTER 2:
Principles of Reason

beneficence

maleficence

marginalized

objective evidence

principle

principles of reason

social ethical issue

subjective evidence

universal

One day you're at school, and two of your friends, Jeff and Andrea, are having a friendly argument before class. Jeff thinks the speed limit on a local highway should be raised from 60 to 70 mph. "We could get to school a lot faster," he says. Andrea disagrees. "We might get to school faster, but raising the speed limit makes the highway more dangerous. There will be more accidents, and more people will be injured or killed. It's not worth risking all that, just to get somewhere a few minutes faster," she says.

Jeff retorts, "I read an article where traffic experts studied this issue, and they found that raising the speed limit by just 10 mph didn't have any effect on the number of accidents." Andrea looks at him and says, "That's crazy, I don't believe that. I read about an expert study that said the exact opposite...there are more accidents, more injuries, and more deaths when the speed limit gets raised."

Jeff rolls his eyes and says, "Look, speed doesn't cause accidents — careless drivers do. If everyone is driving smart and paying attention, it's not going to make a difference whether it's 60 or 70 mph. If someone's not paying attention, they'll be just as dead even if they're driving only 50."

Andrea doesn't get a chance to respond, because the bell rings for the start of class. Later that day, you're thinking back on their conversation and you realize that you're not sure whether you agree with Jeff or Andrea. Both of them felt very strongly about their position. Both of them claimed evidence (expert studies) to support their position. But the evidence was contradictory, and since you didn't actually see or read either study, you don't know if one was more reliable or truthful than the other. You think to yourself, "I'm not sure whether Jeff is right or Andrea is... but they can't both be right, can they?"

TEN UNIVERSAL PRINCIPLES OF CIVILIZATION

Principle of Beneficence (The Golden Rule)

Principle of Non-Contradiction

Principle of Complete Explanation

Principle of Objective Evidence

Principle of Non-Maleficence (The Silver Rule)

Principle of Consistent Ends and Means

Principle of Full Human Potential

Principle of Natural Rights

Principle of the Hierarchy of Rights

Principle of Limits to Freedom

© jophil / iStoc

Throughout our lives, we're constantly witnessing arguments, debates, and controversies, whether it's in world politics or even just in our local school or community. Sometimes it gets very confusing, and we wonder: how do I know who is right, and who is wrong? In this chapter, we're going to explore principles of reason that will help us to analyze arguments and determine which ones are the best. Every argument and every position in this series is based on principles. That's why this series is called *Principles and Choices*.

You may be wondering, "What exactly is a principle anyway?" A **principle** is a basic or fundamental truth that is used to support a line of reasoning, a belief, or a way of behaving. For example, "Cheating is wrong" is a basic principle. It guides our behavior when we do homework or take tests. Principles serve as a kind of a guide in helping us make good choices.

A **principle** is a basic or fundamental truth that is used to support a line of reasoning, a belief, or a way of behaving.

This series will focus on ten universal principles which are all necessary for civilizations to function. Failure to practice even one of them will result in harming human dignity, abusing people, and underestimating our own potential in life. The ten principles are listed in the sidebar on this page. They are also printed with longer descriptions on page 52. You can tear that page out if you like, and save it to use again and again for years to come.

The fact that these principles are "universal" means that they are necessary for any civilization anywhere at any time. Civilizations that abandoned these principles hundreds of years ago caused harm to people. In the same way, civilizations that abandon these principles in our time or in the future will also cause great harm.

PRINCIPLES SERVE AS A GUIDE IN HELPING US MAKE GOOD CHOICES.

These ten principles come from over 2,500 years of logical, scientific, and philosophical reflection on how best to give reasons for what is true. Therefore, they are the best tools we have for understanding what is true, and for defending truth when we are in an argument. There are three particular reasons for the strength of these principles:

1] Without these principles, all of us will be in serious trouble because we would have no legal or political protections against being mistreated. Furthermore, civilization would be in serious trouble because, without legal or political protections, everyone would have to fend for themselves — leading to a deterioration of society.

2] All normal people want these principles applied to them, and they want some order in society and in the marketplace. These principles embody the best of human intelligence and compassion. In technical language, they are **undeniable** by people who are reasonable and responsible.

3] These principles can be used in every proof and every explanation, no matter what topic you are discussing. In technical language, they are **universal**.

That last point deserves an explanation. Remember that principles are fundamental truths that guide people in how to act and make good choices. These principles defend human purpose, happiness, dignity, freedom, and rights. Without them, all of these things are threatened. So these ten principles should never, in any circumstance, be abandoned.

"Oh, come on," you may say. "Every principle can be abandoned in certain areas. Sometimes you need to abandon a principle in order to get things done."

This is a very dangerous position to hold. The problem with giving up on a principle even in a small matter is that the violation makes the use of the principle seem arbitrary to people. In other words, if you can justify violating the principle in one area, why can't someone else justify violating it in another area? They will think that their justification is just as important as you thought yours was.

PRINCIPLES AND DEFINITIONS

The purpose of this four-book series is to teach these principles so that you can form good definitions of reality and develop rational positions on various issues. For example, in order to have an intelligent discussion about the ethics of an issue such as abortion, we have to define words like *personhood*, *ethics*, *freedom*, and *rights*. Good definitions will also help us to analyze other **social ethical issues** such as world hunger, war, prejudice, international poverty, and the oppression of **marginalized** people.

Marginalized — to be pushed off to the side and not given the same rights and protections as the rest of society. Minorities, refugees, the elderly, dying persons, and unborn human beings are examples of frequently marginalized people.

To make sure we have the best definitions, we need principles that are considered undeniable and universal by reasonable and responsible people.

Basic principles will tell us whether or not our definitions of personhood, ethics, freedom, and rights are complete or incomplete, whether they are logical or contradictory, and whether they apply to everyone or only to some people. The best definitions will be as complete, logical, and universally applicable as possible. It is only *after* we have discovered the best possible definitions that we're able to find the best solutions to social ethical issues.

On the other hand, if we form definitions of things *without* good principles to guide us, those definitions will likely become very subjective. Recall the discussion of subjective and objective truth in the last chapter. If we want *objective* truth — if we want to know what something really is, and not just what we "feel" that it is — then we have to follow certain principles that are considered undeniable and universal by reasonable and responsible people. One of these is the *principle of complete explanation*. This principle holds that the best definition will include the most data. When we follow this principle, we won't ignore any data just because that data doesn't fit in with how we "feel" about the thing we are defining.

For example, say Max hates dogs because they stink and slobber all over him. So what if he defined dogs as "smelly, slobbering machines"? If all of society adopted that definition, there would be no responsibility to treat dogs with humaneness or compassion, because machines don't deserve compassion. But Max's definition of dogs violates the principle of

THE BEST DEFINITIONS WILL BE AS COMPLETE, LOGICAL, AND UNIVERSALLY APPLICABLE AS POSSIBLE.

most complete explanation, because dogs are not the sum of their smell and saliva. Max's definition *excludes* many facts about the nature of dogs that most reasonable and responsible people would find relevant.

In this chapter, we are going to define what a human person is. But we cannot have a good definition if we do not start out with good basic principles of how to define something in the first place. By using reliable principles, we can make sure that our definition is truly defining the *human person*, rather than just making up the definition to fit whatever *we feel* about the human person.

It is irresponsible to be satisfied with what you *want* or *feel* to be true, rather than sincerely seeking what is *really* true. This attitude will likely cause you to under-live your life and make choices that are not worthy of you.

Therefore, our first goal in this book is to help you be a great defender of the truth in accordance with the ten principles. Our second goal is for you to be as authentic as possible. Third is for you to use these principles to live the most fulfilling life possible. And finally, we want to equip you to teach these principles to others, so that you might find great purpose in helping others to live an authentic and fulfilling life as well.

The very first principle taught in this series was the *principle of beneficence* or the Golden Rule. We learned it in Book 1, where we studied the four levels of happiness. You may recall that in Level 3 and 4 we find greater happiness by living for the good we

© MissHibiscus / iStockphoto

In Chapter 4, we will focus on applying these principles and definitions to the abortion issue. But these principles and definitions are *universal*— which means they are just as relevant for discussing topics such as capital punishment, nuclear war, immigration, poverty, and hundreds of other important issues. Join in the discussion on our Facebook page to apply these principles to other issues you care about.

can do for other people and for God's kingdom, compared to just living for ourselves. To "do good for others" is also called "beneficence," and it's summed up in the **Golden Rule: "Do unto others as you would have them do unto you."** If you did not have the opportunity to read Book 1, you can find a quick summary of this first principle by using code **PCS222**.

This book describes the three "principles of reason" which help us to discover truth using logic. They include the *principle of non-contradiction*, the *principle of complete explanation*, and the *principle of objective evidence*. We will explain these in greater detail below, and then use them to define personhood in the next chapter.

The final six principles will be covered in Book 3. The first set includes three "principles of ethics," and the last set includes three "principles of justice." They will be used to define freedom, ethics, and human rights. Book 4 will explore the issue of human suffering and will apply all of our principles and definitions to a variety of life issues, such as abortion, human cloning, embryonic stem cell research, and physician-assisted suicide.

THE PRINCIPLE OF NON-CONTRADICTION

Something cannot be both "X" and "not-X" in the same respect at the same place and time.

This is the most basic principle in logic. It is also the most important principle when you are trying to prove anything. It says that something cannot both *be* and *not be* in the same respect at the same place and time. That would be impossible and therefore illogical.

For example, something cannot be a square and a non-square in the same respect at the same place and time. "In the same respect" means in the same substance. So if we have a block of wood, it cannot *be* in the shape of a square and *not be* in the shape of a square at the same place and time. It's either square-shaped or it isn't. It can't be both.

Following this same principle, something cannot be a square and a circle in the same respect at the same place and time, because a circle is a non-square. A square has four inscribed right angles. That means it has four right angles *inside* of it. A circle has zero inscribed right angles. Something cannot have four right angles and zero right angles in the same respect at the same place and time. That's impossible. It's not even possible to imagine a square-circle in your head. Go ahead and try it. Better yet… try drawing a square-circle here:

Whatever you thought or whatever you drew was definitely *not* a square-circle. It might have been half-square and half-circle. Or maybe you drew a square AND a circle, one on top of the other. Or maybe you flipped back and forth really fast in your mind between one and the other. Regardless, you cannot have one object that is both a square and a circle in the same respect (the same substance), at the same place and time. The minute an object has any angles in it, it isn't a circle. And the minute an object has any arcs in it like a circle, it isn't a square. It's something else.

Similarly, something cannot be both blue and not-blue. It cannot be both three feet tall and not three feet tall. It cannot be both a proton and an electron in the same respect at the same place and time. Contradictions are impossible and illogical.

By the way, we're talking only about *objective* facts here, not *subjective* opinions. A dog can be ugly and not-ugly at the same place and time, depending on the varying opinions of the people looking at him. But he cannot be a dog and not be a dog at the same place and time.

Now if someone were to make a claim that was completely contradictory in an argument, you would be justified in saying that his position was illogical, and therefore invalid. Suppose he then said, "Well, who are you to say that contradictions are invalid?" Your answer should be, "If making a contradiction is a valid way to make an argument, then everything you say is both true and false at the same time." At that point, you can't have a conversation about anything anymore, because nothing will make sense. Everything "is" and "is not" at the same time. The philosopher Aristotle said that if you think this way, you basically reduce yourself to the status of a vegetable, because you can't even think of anything meaningful within your own mind.[1]

This principle is essential not only in the world of logic, but also in our practical lives. Imagine that you are following directions for assembling a bicycle and the instructions say, "Insert a safety bolt in the last hole on piece #14, but DO NOT insert a safety bolt in the last hole on piece #14." You will probably be very confused, and might call the manufacturer to find out what you are supposed to do. Obviously, you cannot both "insert a bolt" and "not insert a bolt" at the same time in the same hole. Logical contradictions make it impossible to do anything.

THE PRINCIPLE OF COMPLETE EXPLANATION

The best explanation is the one which accounts for the most data.

This principle means that if there are two (or more) opinions about something, the best opinion is going to be the one that includes the most information, has the most evidence, and answers the most questions logically and coherently. The *best* explanation about anything will be the most *complete* explanation — one that does not overlook or ignore any data.

For example, say Max and Christopher are standing on a seashore, arguing about whether the earth is round or flat. Max points to the horizon and says, "See… it's totally flat. You can see the end, and then it stops."

Christopher asks, "Well then why doesn't all the water fall off the end of the earth and drain out?"

"Because there's a retaining wall that holds it in," answers Max.

"Well, why can't I see it?" says Christopher.

"I don't know. Maybe it's invisible. Or maybe it's too far away for you to see. Or maybe God just holds it up."

Christopher is not convinced that any of these answers are logical or coherent. So he gets in a boat and sails away toward the horizon. One year later, Christopher comes back and rushes to visit his friend Max.

"You were wrong," says Christopher. "Water does not fall off the end of the earth, because the earth is round. I sailed all the way around it. I have brought back maps and charts of my journey to show you. And I can even take you with me on a second journey to prove that it is round."

But Max ignores Christopher's data, glances out over the sea, and says, "It looks flat to me. It must be flat."

Who has the better opinion? The vast majority of people would say that Christopher's opinion is objectively better than Max's because Christopher has included more information, has more evidence to support his opinion, and has answered more questions more logically and coherently than Max has.

In other words, Christopher has accounted for more data than Max.

Most people would NOT argue that being able to explain more and having more evidence is NOT better. That wouldn't make any sense. If adding more evidence to an argument doesn't make it stronger, then evidence doesn't matter, which means that subjective opinions are all we have left. As we saw in the first chapter, subjective opinions are arbitrary and will never lead us to objective truth. The Greek philosopher Plato said this would be like each of us living in our own little shadow worlds, never venturing out into the world of real light.

Now, of course, the principle of complete explanation can be quite inconvenient. Trying to get the most complete explanation about anything takes time and commitment. But ignoring this principle will make life even more inconvenient in the long run. Let's say you ask for directions to the theater and you tell your friend, "I don't want the most complete explanation, and I don't care if you leave out a few turns. Just sum it up in two sentences." You will probably end up lost.

You may have heard this old saying: "There are far more errors of omission than commission." This means that when we come up with mistaken explanations for things, it is most often because we have left out important data (errors of omission), *not* that we have put the data together incorrectly (errors of commission). Most of the time people leave out important data unintentionally. But

THERE ARE FAR MORE ERRORS OF OMISSION THAN COMMISSION.

sometimes they leave things out on purpose in order to deceive people, and so the old saying we mentioned above is sometimes expressed this way: "There are far more lies of omission than commission." We have to be on the lookout for data which is left out — whether it is intentional or not.

THE PRINCIPLE OF OBJECTIVE EVIDENCE

For a claim to be reasonable, you must provide evidence that can be verified by others.

Imagine your friend Meghan comes to you one day and says, "Little green Martians visit me in my bedroom every night. One time they even abducted me and brought me aboard their spaceship." You say, "Wow, really? I want to see this. I'll come over tonight." So she answers, "Well, you can't. I'm the only one who can see them." You reply, "Okay. Just tell them to say something to me," and she answers, "I'm the only one who can hear them." So finally you say, "Well ask them to communicate to me in some way. Maybe they can move furniture around in the room or something." And she replies, "I'm sorry. They're very shy, and they won't do anything for anybody unless I'm all alone."

You would be right to seriously doubt your friend's claim.

The last principle we discussed was about the *quantity* of evidence. It stated that the more data you have, the better your position.

This principle deals with the *quality* of evidence. Some evidence is strong and some is weak. A video of a woman murdering her neighbor is better evidence of the woman's guilt than a co-worker who says, "I heard her say she was going to kill him."

The best kind of evidence is evidence that other people can verify. The people on the jury can look at the video and see the woman murdering her neighbor. If they can verify the identities, and an expert can verify that the video has not been altered, they will likely come to the same conclusion that the woman murdered him.

But the people on the jury were not present when the co-worker had this supposed conversation with the woman. It would be difficult for the jury to know whether the co-worker is telling the truth, whether she heard correctly, and whether she is remembering the conversation accurately. The accused woman would simply have to say, "I never said that," and no one would be able to verify whether her claim is true or false.

Another way of stating this principle is "arbitrarily asserted, arbitrarily denied." The word "arbitrary" means that an action or statement is based on individual preference or convenience, rather than on necessity or reality.

This means if you make an arbitrary claim that something is true, someone else can just as easily make an arbitrary claim that it is *not* true. For example, let's suppose you blurt out, "Life exists on other planets! I just know it!" Someone else could blurt out, "No it doesn't! I just know it!" Neither one of you has made a very good argument, so no one wins this debate. The conversation has come to a dead end.

Now, this principle does not mean that if someone has a private religious experience, it is not real or true. Nor does it mean that your own private thoughts are not real or true. But these things can only be verified by the individual who experienced them, so there is not enough evidence to prove them publicly.

Evidence that can be verified only by one individual is called "subjective evidence." Evidence that can be verified by anyone who is able to use their five senses, or by anyone who is intelligent enough to follow a logical argument or perceive a self-evident truth is called "objective evidence."

CONCLUSION

All three of the principles of reason outlined above will help you to discover what is objectively true. Every form of logic, science, and mathematics depends on these three principles, and the rest of this course will depend on applying them thoroughly and correctly.

In the next chapter, we will use these three principles to develop the most complete and correct definition possible of a human person.

Use code **PCS223** to access study tools for this chapter.

CHAPTER 3:
Defining the Human Person

The term "human being" refers to any being of human origin, and is generally not a controversial term. However, the term "human *person*" does stir up controversy. It refers to a human being who possesses rights that deserve to be protected under the law.

There are some people who believe that not all human beings are human persons. They believe that certain groups of human beings do not have any rights that need to be protected or recognized by government. This is a very dangerous belief which can lead to many kinds of discrimination and abuse. Consequently, it is important to define "human person" as carefully, accurately, and completely as possible. In this chapter, we will use all three of the principles of reason from Chapter 2 to develop the best definition of a human person.

Cultures that settle for very poor definitions of "human person" will usually end up seriously violating the human rights of many people. For example, let's imagine our society decided that the word "human person" includes only individuals over the age of 20. Using that definition, we would have to exclude millions of young people from most legal rights and protections. This would unfairly subject them to abuse, slavery, oppression, and murder without any legal recourse. Obviously, no one would want that to happen. The definition of a human person must be objective, not subjective; and therefore, it must not violate any of the principles of reason we have learned.

History is filled with examples of powerful groups of people who used narrow and subjective definitions of "human person" to exclude whole groups of weaker and more vulnerable people. They used these subjective definitions to oppress, enslave, and murder thousands, and even millions, of people.

KEY TERMS

agape love

essence

human being

human person

nominal definition

objective definition

real definition

subjective definition

telos

transcend

Subjective Definitions of "Human Persons"

Africans	"They [Negroes] should be and are considered an inferior class of beings, who have been subjugated by the dominant race, and whether emancipated or not, have no rights...." (*Dred Scott v. Sandford*, 60 U.S. 393, 1857)
Slaves	"In the eyes of the law... the slave is not a person." (*Bailey v. Poindexter's Ex'or*, 14 Grattan 432, 1858)
Native Americans	"An Indian is not a person within the meaning of the Constitution... Congress may prevent an Indian leaving his reservation, and while he is on a reservation it may deprive him of his liberty, his property, his life... Congress may break its treaties with him as it may repeal a statute." (George F. Canfield, "The Legal Position of the Indian," *The American Law Review*. 15:28, January 1881)
Women	"The statutory word 'person' did not in these circumstances include women." (Cited in *Commonwealth v. Welosky*, 177 *North Eastern Reporter* 660, 1931)
Jews	"The Jew is not a human being. He is an appearance of putrescence." (Supreme Party Judge Walter Buch, *Deutsche Justiz*, October 21, 1938)

Real human persons were severely harmed by these bad definitions. Some who did not qualify as "persons" were enslaved or forced into labor. Some were exterminated in concentration camps or subjected to cruel physical and psychological experiments. Some were made into second-class citizens, denied full participation in society, and denied basic civil and human rights. Others were persecuted, tortured, raped, and murdered. All of this was done with the approval of people in positions of authority whose primary purpose should have been the protection of less powerful individuals.

In order to avoid repeating these atrocities in our own time or in the future, it is necessary to construct the very best, most complete, and most inclusive definition of a human person possible, and then to courageously stand by that definition, no matter what the consequences.

HOW TO DEFINE SOMETHING

Imagine you were from the early 20th century, and you suddenly were transported to the present moment. You enter a dimly lit room and find a mobile phone lying on the table, but you have no idea what it is. So you pick it up and press a button, and the screen lights up. You think to yourself, "Wow! A flashlight shaped like a little box!" And you use it to find your way out of the room.

Using the mobile phone as a flashlight certainly serves your need at the moment, but "a flashlight" is a very poor definition for a mobile phone. Without understanding what it really is, you would completely miss the fascinating 21st century technology that allows you to have real-time voice conversations with people who are far away, hold video chats, take photographs, surf the web, send texts and emails, play games, read books, and download thousands of apps allowing you to do all sorts of things. What a waste!

This section will show you how to avoid making this kind of mistake, by laying out a strategy for how to define something.

There are two different kinds of definitions: nominal definitions and real definitions.

A **nominal definition** assigns a name to a thing. When you were a child, you learned that vessels that could float in water and carry people were called "boats." Today, if someone pointed to such a vessel in the water and said, "What is that?" you would answer, "That is a boat."

Assigning names to objects is the basis of language itself. Without assigning names, we could not communicate. However, nominal definitions don't tell you anything about the object you are trying to define. A name is just a group of letters on paper or a vocal sound or sign that we customarily use when referring to a specific thing. We could decide at any time to change the word, the sound, or the sign we use to refer to a "boat." But that would not change the *essence* of the boat. For example, if you had a friend from France and you both were looking at a boat, she would call it "le bateau," while you would call it "boat." But it's still the same object. Boats are real objects that still exist even if you change the name you give to it.

A **real definition** tries to get to the essence of the thing you are defining. "Essence" means the intrinsic nature of the thing — or what the thing is at its very heart and core. Aristotle called this the *"to ti ēn einai."* This phrase means, "What it was meant to be" at its fullest potential or development.

With a nominal definition, we are imposing a word onto the thing. With a real definition, we don't impose anything. We observe the object, study it, learn from it, and discover what it truly is.

Aristotle, who lived 2,400 years ago, was not satisfied with nominal definitions. He wanted to know what things were at their very essence — at their core. He wanted a *complete explanation* of things. Aristotle understood that it was essential to have a complete explanation of what something was before you could really understand its uses, value, and purpose. So Aristotle developed four different ways to uncover the real definition of a thing. His method is still valid today, because it follows the principle of complete explanation.

> **"ESSENCE" IS WHAT A THING IS AT ITS VERY HEART AND CORE.**

Use code **PCS231** to read Aristotle's actual words for explaining these four steps.

FOUR STEPS TO UNCOVERING A REAL DEFINITION
(A "Complete Explanation")

The principle of complete explanation states that the best definition is the one which accounts for the most data. In order to do that, we need to account for four different types of data:

1] A complete **physical description**. This can include its various components, appearance, size, shape, feel, smell, sound, taste, and observable activities. (Aristotle called this the "material cause.")

2] List of all its different **powers**. What are its potentials? What is it capable of, or what would it be capable of if given enough time to grow and develop to its fullest potential? (Aristotle called this the "formal cause.")

3] The **conditions** that are necessary for the thing to exist and to turn its powers on. What does it need in order to exist? What does it need to actually make use of its powers? What does it need to develop to its fullest potential? (Aristotle called this the "efficient cause.")

4] The fulfillment of its powers, or what its **full purpose** is. What is its final end or final goal? What is its fullest stage of development? (Aristotle called this the "final cause.")

If we could carry out each of these steps perfectly, we would have a complete definition of whatever it was we were trying to define.

This is not an easy thing to do. For example, it is difficult to follow each step when we are trying to define something as complex as a living organism, let alone a human being. It seems like there is always more to discover about ourselves. But the purpose of human inquiry is to try to understand as much as we can about things. So our goal is to reach the most complete definition possible with the data we currently have. Even though we may not end up with a completely and absolutely *perfect* definition of human persons, we certainly don't want to leave anything out if we can avoid it. We want the *most* complete explanation *possible*. Then, if new data is discovered in the future, we will want to include that data in our definition.

© matka_Wariatka / iStockphoto

TESTING OUR THEORY ON AN ACORN

Let us assume we are attempting to define an acorn.

PHYSICAL DESCRIPTION

The first thing we will notice is the acorn's physical characteristics (step one). The acorn is about an inch in height, oval-shaped, green and brown in color, hard, and has a bumpy cap on top. It doesn't have any observable activities. It just sits there. But this first step cannot be all there is to defining an acorn because it is incomplete. The first step doesn't really tell us anything about the object we are defining, except how our senses perceive it. We need to go deeper.

POWERS

The next thing we must do is identify all of the acorn's powers (step two). By studying it, we will discover that the acorn has various vegetative powers. It can absorb water and nutrients, and let out waste. Once it is in soil, it can grow. It can perform photosynthetic activity (it can absorb energy from the sun and use it to make carbohydrates). It can reproduce. These powers really exist in the acorn right now, even before it has been planted and watered in warm, nutrient-rich earth. These powers are a real part of the acorn, but they are lying dormant. How do we know this? Because if certain conditions are met, those powers will start to act.

CONDITIONS

So what are all the conditions that are necessary to turn on all of the acorn's powers (step three)? And what are the conditions that are necessary for it to even exist? First, the acorn needs an oak tree on which to grow. Furthermore, just because the acorn exists and has powers does not mean that those powers will turn on all by themselves and do something. Before an acorn can photosynthesize, grow, and reproduce, it needs to be planted in soil. It needs a certain temperature range, some water and nutrients, the right amount of carbon dioxide, and some sunlight.

All of this gives us more valuable data about the acorn. It tells us that an acorn is a complex organism with layers and layers of parts that make it up. It tells us that acorns are sensitive to temperature, and that they are "water absorbers," "nutrient and carbon dioxide absorbers," "sunlight absorbers," and much more. But we still have an incomplete definition because conditions and powers point to even more data.

FULL PURPOSE

When all of the conditions are met for the acorn to exist, and when all of the conditions are present which are necessary to turn its powers on, those powers do not just start performing random and aimless activities. The acorn starts to grow like an oak tree. Not like a baboon… not like a rose bush. Like an oak tree. Why? How does it do that? Written within the genetic code of every acorn is a sort of "map" guiding it toward a particular end. In other words, all of the powers of the acorn are being directed toward a final goal — it's full purpose, or what Aristotle called its *telos*.

> Telos (pronounced *TAY-loss*) is the Greek word for "end," "final goal," or "full purpose." The Greeks had another term for this: "*to ti ēn einai*" (pronounced *tah tee ain ain-eye*). Literally, this means, "what it was to be" or "what it was meant to be."

YOU HAVE FULL VALUE EVEN BEFORE YOU REACH YOUR FULL PURPOSE.

What Aristotle meant by *telos* was the point at which a certain thing reaches its fullest stage of development — the fullest form of its power. For the acorn, this would be a fully developed oak tree. Written within the genetic code of every acorn is information that directs it toward the final goal of becoming an oak tree.

Now, this information is not just knowledge that you have in your mind. This is very real information within the acorn itself, and it has the power to direct the development of the acorn towards oak tree.

This real information gives the acorn "oak tree value" even before it has fully actualized itself as a tree. It contains all the information necessary to make itself fully operational as an oak tree. It just needs time and the right conditions to develop the powers it already has.

To understand why that last point is so important, let's say you have a friend named Kaylee, and you are very excited to show her the new laptop you just purchased moments ago. But before you even get it out of the box, Kaylee leaps up, grabs the whole thing from your hands, and smashes it several times on the ground. When you open the box, you find that your computer has been destroyed.

"What in the world did you do that for?" you shout.

"Didn't you see that huge spider?" she says. "Good thing I smashed it before it got away."

"But you just destroyed my laptop!" you cry.

© Photolyric / iStockphoto

Now, what if Kaylee were to say to you, "Oh, don't worry. You never took it out of the box. It's never been booted up and you hadn't loaded any software on it yet. It's never done anything. It wasn't a real laptop. It was just a potential laptop." Would that make you feel better?

Obviously not — because it *wasn't* a potential laptop. It was a real laptop. Even though it was brand new and hadn't done anything yet, all of the information necessary to make it fully operational as a laptop was already there in the laptop, existing as a real power. That information made it very valuable.

THE DEFINITION...

Getting back to our acorn example, we now have a far more complete definition of an acorn than the mere observation that the acorn is small, round, and hard. **An acorn is a living organism which contains a real and existing power to direct its own development toward oak tree, and will do so if all the proper conditions are met.**

DEFINING A HUMAN PERSON

If you were to try to explain to a four-year-old child what a human person was, you would probably point to some different people — an old man, a teenage girl, a mother and her young son, and say, "See? Those are all human persons."

That would be a *nominal* definition. The four-year-old would easily grasp the point that "human person" does not refer to a dog, a cat, or a bug. It refers to a particular kind of being that resembles you and her.

But as we saw in the sections above, a nominal definition is not enough. It hasn't revealed anything about the *nature* of a human being. The child is missing a lot of information that would be essential if our goal is to prevent her from excluding anybody from the category of human personhood in the future.

At this point, some people complain that the task before us is going to be difficult and controversial. They are tempted to say, "Can't we just agree that a human person is whatever we want it to be?" But we've already seen the danger of using subjective definitions. History is filled with examples of cultures that did this, and the results were catastrophic. Human persons are an objective reality. It is important to know *objectively* what a human person is so that no real person is ever excluded from that category again.

Remember, if we're following an objective process, we can't simply *impose* a definition on human persons. Rather, we *discover* what a human person is through observation. We need to construct the very best, most complete, and most inclusive definition of a human person possible.

We need a *real* definition — a complete explanation.

PHYSICAL DESCRIPTION

To get there, we start with a physical description. But it soon becomes obvious how subjective that is. We all look different. We have different sizes, shapes, and appearances. There are some similarities, of course, but these can change. Most people walk upright, but some don't (such as infants). Most people have two eyes, two legs, two arms, and hair...but others don't. If we try to find a physical characteristic of human beings that is universal and applies to everyone, we find there are always exceptions.

Digging deeper, science has allowed us to identify the full human genome using a DNA sequencer. This data satisfies the principle of objective evidence, because it is publicly accessible. Anyone can use a DNA sequencer to map out the human genome.

Although there will be differences within the basic genetic structure of human beings, we all share the same essential structure and sequence of chromosomes and genes. It is different from apes, monkeys, dolphins, and every other species — each of which has its own unique genetic structure.

POWERS

There are many powers that human beings have in common with animals: we take in energy, let out waste, and grow. We reproduce, experience pleasure and pain, and move ourselves from one place to another.

But human beings have powers that animals do not have. If you studied the first book in this series (*Identity and Values*), you know that human beings desire perfect, unconditional, and absolute Truth, Love, Justice, Beauty, and Unity.

By using the **principle of objective evidence**, we can see that this desire is not subjective. It is very real. All human beings seem to share this desire. Abundant evidence for this appears over thousands of years of literature, drama, art, music, architecture, mathematics, science, media, and social media. It is shared in people's conversations, their journals, their thoughts, and their expressions. This desire is expressed by millions of people in their homes, schools, workplaces, and churches. It is likely that most reasonable and responsible people you speak to will verify that they share this desire, even if they don't use the same words to describe it.

Furthermore, human beings are able to meditate on this desire, and then to act on it. Human beings have the power

Agape is far more than physical

Some scientists argue that the **power to love** can be traced to chemicals, DNA, and even body odor. [K] But these scientists are usually equating love with physical sexual arousal — and that is not the kind of love we mean in this series.

Agape love is not an involuntary biological reaction to sexual arousal. *Agape* is the ability to choose joy, peace, patience, kindness, generosity, goodness, gentleness, compassion, empathy, faithfulness, self-control, courage, prudence, chastity, and other virtues. *Agape* empowers us to choose these virtues even when it costs us, and is contrary to our biophysical instincts. It allows us to choose the good of others over our own good. While there is evidence that certain physical changes in the body can be detected when we are engaging in these qualities, there is absolutely no evidence that our ability or desire to choose these qualities (or reject them) is reducible to a physical part. These qualities seem to transcend ("rise above") physical reality.

to respond to this desire through acts of love, gentleness, humbleness, forgiveness, mercy, peacemaking, generosity, patience, kindness, and compassion. Human beings can experience empathy. In short, we have the capacity for *agape* love.

No other form of life on earth shares the human capacity for *agape* love. While many animals can participate in deeply affectionate love, there is no empirical scientific evidence that they exhibit a self-sacrificial and empathetic *agape* love. For example, if you and your cat have not eaten for two days and you find a piece of ham, you might, out of compassion, give it to your cat to eat. But she would not do the same for you.

So, where does the power for *agape* love come from? Ancient Greek philosophers observed that the power to love proves the existence of the soul. The human soul is the non-physical part of ourselves — the spiritual part of ourselves — that contains our non-physical (spiritual) power. The fact that we have abilities that are not physical proves that there must be a part of ourselves that is not merely physical.

WHAT MAKES HUMANS DIFFERENT FROM ALL OTHER BEINGS ON EARTH?

No other species seems to have these powers. Nor do they appear to have the human desire for the perfect and the infinite. Because there is no evidence that other life forms share these powers, it is reasonable to believe that only human beings possess these powers. Therefore, if we want the most complete explanation possible, these powers should be included in an objective definition of the human person.

Use code **PCS232** to read about scientific studies exploring the existence of the human soul.

There is abundant philo-
sophical and scientific
evidence that we also need God
as a condition for our existence.
If you are interested in seeing this
evidence, use code **PCS233**.

**List other conditions that are
necessary for the human person
to exist.** What about other conditions that are necessary to turn on
our uniquely human powers?

_____

_____

_____

_____

_____

_____

_____

_____

_____

_____

_____

_____

_____

_____

_____

CONDITIONS

Like the acorn, human beings need water, nutrition, and a certain temperature range. But there are other conditions we need that acorns do not need. Human beings need companionship. We need family and friends. We need love, and the touch of others. We need to be forgiven. Some studies have shown that without the relationship of other human beings, people can become deeply mentally disturbed.

FULL PURPOSE

What is the full purpose of the human person? What is our _telos_? When we were considering the purpose for the computer, the mobile phone, and the acorn, we had to ask what would fulfill their highest powers. The same principle is true with the human person.

The highest power of a human person is to find fulfillment through perfect, unconditional, and infinite Truth, Love, Goodness, Beauty, and Unity. We know this to be true because of the proofs given in Book 1 on human happiness, success, quality of life, and love. Nothing less will satisfy us. So in order to have the most _complete_ definition of a human person possible, we have to include this fullest stage of human development.

Now you might say, "Wait a minute…wouldn't that mean you're a human person only when you have _reached_ that fullest stage of development?"

If that were true, then most of us could _not_ be considered human persons for much of our lives. At any given time, many people are _not_ finding fulfillment through perfect, unconditional, and infinite Truth, Love, Goodness, Beauty, and Unity. Some people are too young to understand it. Some people are not aware of it. Other people are rejecting it. Some people are asleep. There are many distractions in this world, and most of us experience the crises of Levels 1, 2, and 3 many times throughout our lives. Are we going to exclude all of these groups from human personhood because they are not, at that moment, _using_ their highest power?

If we want a _complete_ definition, then we cannot exclude some groups from personhood just because their highest power is not in use at a particular moment. If we do that, we're overlooking real data. Recall that there is real information present in the human person — like a map or blueprint — which guides the powers toward their fulfillment. That information really exists inside the human being, and it has real value — infinite value.

What makes you a human person is not simply the fact that you are _using_ your power to find final fulfillment through God. What makes you a human person is that you _have_ the power within you to find final fulfillment through God, and there is guiding information, or a "map" inside you that helps to direct your power toward that end. It's the same argument for the computer, the mobile

WE HAVE THE POWER TO FIND TRUTH, LOVE, GOODNESS, BEAUTY AND UNITY.

© franckreporter / iStockphoto

WHAT DEFINES THE COMPUTER IS ITS POWER TO COMPUTE AND THE MAP INSIDE WHICH GUIDES IT IN ITS COMPUTATIONS WHEN IT'S TURNED ON. THE ACTUAL STATUS OF WHETHER THE COMPUTER IS COMPUTING IS IRRELEVANT TO THE DEFINITION OF WHAT IT IS.

phone, and the acorn. What defines the computer is its *power* to compute and the map inside which guides it in its computations when it's turned on. The actual status of whether the computer is computing is irrelevant to the definition of *what* it is.

THE DEFINITION...

We now have an objective definition of the human person, which is as complete as possible using all of the data that is available to us:

A human person is a living being that contains a real and existing power to direct its own development toward fulfillment through perfect, unconditional, and infinite Truth, Love, Goodness, Beauty, and Unity, and will do so if all the proper conditions are met.

This definition of the human person is reasonable and responsible because it follows all of the principles of reason that we learned in Chapter 2:

1] This definition is **complete** *(principle of complete explanation)* because it does not ignore any of the unique and distinctive characteristics of human beings.

2] This definition is **objective** *(principle of objective evidence)* because it includes only data that everyone else has access to and can verify for themselves.

3] There is nothing in the definition that contradicts itself. Therefore, the definition does not violate the *principle of non-contradiction.*

YOUR CHOICE

At this point, you have to make a choice about what to believe. You have the freedom to accept this definition, or reject it.

If you accept the principles of reason, it will be virtually impossible to reject the above definition of the human person, because it is the most objective and the most complete definition possible. Any other definition will probably violate one or more of the principles of reason.

For example, Peter Singer is a professor of Bioethics at Princeton University. He claims that the term "person" should be limited to *only* "a being who is capable of anticipating the future, of having wants and desires for the future." [L]

In order to qualify for Peter Singer's definition of a human person, you would be required to have advanced brain function. He excludes newborn infants, babies who are not yet self-aware, and people with severe brain abnormalities, injuries, and illnesses. This exclusion allows Singer to say that "killing a newborn baby is never equivalent to killing a person." [M]

But Singer's definition is a serious violation of the principle of complete explanation, because it ignores essential data about human persons. His definition excludes the really existing unique *power* within the human person to seek fulfillment through perfect, unconditional, and infinite Truth, Love, Goodness, Beauty, and Unity. This power exists before the human being is capable of anticipating the future. It exists even before the human being is self-aware. Anticipation of the future and self-awareness occur only when the powers are fully actualized under the right conditions. But just because the infant has not yet reached the stage of development where she can fully use this power, does not mean the infant lacks this power inside herself. To kill an infant because she is not yet using her powers would be similar to Kaylee smashing your computer because you hadn't yet loaded it with software.

So why would a reasonable and responsible person accept Peter Singer's narrow and incomplete definition of a human person? If you accept the principles of reason, why would you want to exclude *any* human being from the definition of human person?

Nevertheless, you could choose to reject the principles of reason, and accept a definition of the human person that is based on subjective and incomplete data, like Peter Singer's. But if you do this, you will open the door to many other subjective and incomplete definitions of the human person. What will your defense be in the future if someone uses a subjective definition that excludes *you*?

WHAT IF SOMEONE USES A SUBJECTIVE DEFINITION THE OF HUMAN PERSON THAT EXCLUDES YOU?

CHAPTER 4:
Application to Social Issues

CHAPTER FOUR
KEY TERMS

arbitrary

Dr. Jerome Lejeune

empirical

fertilization

fertilized egg

fetus

human genome

inferior

legitimize

soul

subordinate

zygote

Suppose that a race of aliens from another planet has been secretly monitoring Earth for years. One day they discover the cure for cancer and, being a benevolent race, they decide to share it with us. But not wanting to frighten us with their bizarre appearance, they implant information about the cure into the brains of twenty of their infant members, load them onto a spacecraft tended by nanny robots, and send them into space on a journey to Earth. Their hope is that we will think their infants are cute and nurture them into adulthood, at which time the mature aliens can then access data embedded in their brains and share it with us, ending cancer forever. One month later the ship lands on earth, near the city where you live.

Unfortunately, the infant aliens don't appear as cute as the mission planners had hoped. They have the appearance of lumpy tadpoles the size of large watermelons, and, being infants, they are not yet able to communicate. When they are deposited from the ship by the nanny robots, they begin wriggling around on the ground like huge worms.

Terrified by the strange appearance and awkward activities of the writhing aliens, the mayor of the city proclaims that they are wild alien beasts, and says that the best thing to do is to kill them all right away.

"Wait a minute," you say. "These things came to us in a very advanced spacecraft, and they do not appear to be aggressive. This would seem to suggest that they are creatures capable of organized thought and advanced activity. Perhaps they have come on a mission of peace. Maybe we should study them a bit more before we decide what they are and how we should treat them." *cont'd...*

© frenta / Fotolia

In 1857, the United States Supreme Court decided that Black human beings were not persons because their bodies were not white. In 1973, the United States Supreme Court decided that unborn human beings were not persons because their bodies were not fully developed. Compare these two decisions. How are they the same? How are they different?

_____

_____

_____

_____

_____

_____

_____

_____

_____

_____

_____

_____

_____

_____

Enter code **PCS241** to read the actual *Dred Scott* decision, declaring that Black people were not fully human.

The mayor eyes you suspiciously and says, "Are you kidding? While we waste time, these things may be preparing to eat us alive, or emit a deadly gas to wipe out our race. In order to save time, why don't we just agree that they're peaceful creatures for you, but wild beasts for the rest of us. You can go home and we'll kill them. Nobody will force you to participate."

"That violates the most basic principle of logic," you say.

How would you finish this argument using the principle of non-contradiction?

Unmoved by your logic, the mayor retorts, "Logic, schmogic. Just look at them, writhing there. They're the ugliest things I've ever seen. And even if they're harmless, they're not doing anything useful by just sitting there wiggling around. It's not the same thing as killing a person or something."

"But you don't know anything about them," you say. "You're trying to define them just based on what you see."

How would you finish this argument using the principle of complete explanation?

By now the mayor is frustrated and exasperated. He waves his fist in the air and yells at you. "I'm telling you, they're dangerous. I've got a bad feeling about the whole thing."

"Mayor, with all due respect," you say, "I appreciate your feelings, but you can't expect the rest of us to agree they're dangerous just because you've got a bad feeling."

How would you finish this argument using the principle of objective evidence?

Unfortunately, the mayor has succeeded in frightening all the other people who have gathered. In a terrified frenzy, they push you out of the way and kill the aliens, unwittingly destroying the cure for cancer in the process.

Although the story above is just a fantasy of science fiction, it is a tragic fact that history has frequently judged human beings to be non-persons because of how they look or how they act. Many innocent and vulnerable persons with untold gifts and talents have been lost to abuses of the worst kind because of the unjust judgments of others.

For example, in 1857, the United States Supreme Court decided that Black human beings were a "subordinate and inferior class of beings." [N]

Subordinate means to be under the power or authority of someone else. Inferior means to be lower in quality or value.

Thus, they were denied the status of persons because their bodies were not white, and because there was no evidence in the Constitution that Black human beings should be considered "persons." This decision was based on *arbitrary criteria*. In other words, the measurement used by the Supreme Court had absolutely nothing to do with what it really means to be a human person.

Remember from Chapter 3 that a "human person" is "**a living being which contains a real and existing power to direct its own development toward fulfillment through perfect, unconditional, and infinite Truth, Love, Goodness, Beauty, and Unity, and will do so if all the proper conditions are met.**"

To simplify this definition, we will refer to Truth, Love, Goodness, Beauty, and Unity as "the five transcendentals" as we did in Chapter 1 of Book 1.

A "transcendental" goes beyond (or "transcends") physical reality. It is real, but is not physical or material. Your soul is a transcendental reality. So are truth, love, and justice. For example, "justice" is not a tangible object that you can understand with your five senses. You cannot touch or taste justice. Yet you know when you are being treated unjustly.

It was true in 1857, as it is today, that black human beings have as much a yearning for the five transcendentals as do white, brown, and other-colored human beings. The art, music, language, prayer, literature, and social customs of Blacks gave plenty of evidence that they are equal to persons of other colors in their hunger for God and in their capacity for *agape* love.

The color of our skin does not change the status of our personhood, or the worth and value we have as human beings. And the fact that the Constitution does not specifically mention Black people does not mean they are not human persons. It just means that the Constitution doesn't mention them. There is nothing spelled out in the Constitution about Japanese or Mexican people either, but that does not mean they are not human persons.

In 1973, the United States Supreme Court wrote a decision that was strikingly similar to the *Dred Scott* case in its approach to defining human persons. In the *Roe v. Wade* decision, the Court claimed that unborn human beings were not persons because their bodies were not fully developed, and because the Justices could find nothing in past Court cases that said unborn humans were persons.

THE "REAL AND EXISTING POWER" IN THE DEFINITION OF THE HUMAN PERSON IS SOMETIMES CALLED A "SOUL." THE CONCEPT OF A "SOUL" IS NOT A RELIGIOUS CREATION. ARISTOTLE LOGICALLY ARGUED FOR THE EXISTENCE OF THE HUMAN SOUL NEARLY 2,500 YEARS AGO, USING PHILOSOPHICAL REASONING.

The rest of this chapter will lay out an argument against *Roe v. Wade*, using the principles of reason, and our objective and complete definition of the human person.

ABORTION AND THE PRINCIPLE OF NON-CONTRADICTION

Something cannot be both X and not-X in the same respect at the same place and time.

The following is an example of an exchange we might hear between people who disagree on abortion.

Emma: Abortion should be illegal because it kills a human person.

Robert: The fetus is not a human person.

Emma: Yes it is.

Robert: No it isn't.

Emma: Yes. It is.

Robert: NO. It ISN'T.

Emma: Yeah…it really is.

Robert: Okay, look. We'll never agree on this. So let's just say it's a person for you but not for me.

Emma: Okay, fine. Whatever.

While this may get Robert and Emma out of an uncomfortable conversation, their conclusion is completely illogical — not to mention unjust to the fetus, whose status as a human person has nothing to do with whether or not Robert and Emma agree.

According to the principle of non-contradiction, the fetus cannot be both a "person" and a "non-person" in the same respect at the same place and time, depending on who is looking at it. It either is a human person, or it is not.

As we learned from Chapters 1 and 3, personhood is not an opinion, or a decision, or a compromise. It's an objective fact. We can learn the definition of "human person" by identifying all the powers, conditions, and full purpose of human persons. Then we can determine whether something is or isn't a human person by applying this complete and objective definition and seeing if it fits.

When Robert and Emma decide to give up and agree to a contradiction, they avoid pursuing the truth. This wouldn't be a big deal if they were discussing tomatoes; but they are discussing something that may be a human person with intrinsic worth. Their conclusions will have a significant impact on the future of something that may actually be a some*body* with unconditional value.

This violation of the principle of non-contradiction does not just occur in private discussions about abortion. It also occurs in court decisions, laws and regulations, and even scientific discourse.

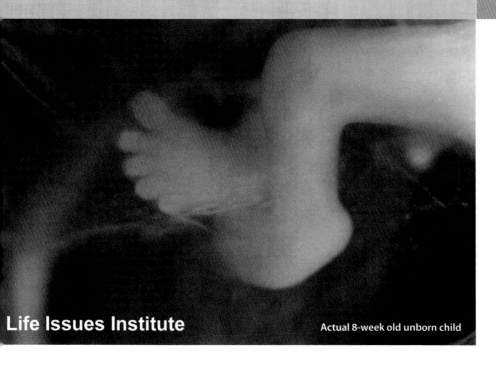

Life Issues Institute

Actual 8-week old unborn child

On April 1, 2004, President George W. Bush signed into law the Unborn Victims of Violence Act of 2004, also known as "Laci and Conner's Law." This federal law protects unborn children from assault and murder outside of the abortion context. You can access the text of the law using code **PCS243**.

For example, many states have laws that grant personhood and rights to unborn children under certain circumstances, such as when parents make an unborn child the beneficiary in their will, or when a person sues someone for injuries he sustained when he was still a baby in the womb, or when a state files homicide charges against someone who attacks a pregnant woman resulting in the death of her unborn child. And yet, at the same time, these same states recognize abortion as a right, thereby claiming that the unborn child is not a person and has no rights.

So in other words, the child is a person with rights of inheritance if her parents name her in their will, but that same child is not a person and doesn't even have the right to life if her parents want to get an abortion.

AN UNBORN CHILD IS EITHER A PERSON OR HE IS NOT A PERSON. HE CANNOT BE BOTH AT THE SAME TIME.

She's a person with the right to life if someone kills her against her mother's wishes, but she's not a person and has no rights if her mother wishes to get an abortion.

In science, biologists recognize that at the *moment* of fertilization (the union of the sperm and the egg), an unborn child has a full human genome — which means that it can't be anything other than a human being. And yet, some biologists also claim that the unborn child is not a human being until it implants in the mother's womb — several days *after* fertilization.

These are all serious violations of the principle of non-contradiction. An unborn child is either a person or he is not a person. He cannot be both at the same time.

ABORTION AND THE PRINCIPLE OF COMPLETE EXPLANATION

The best explanation is the one which accounts for the most data.

Another argument we sometimes hear in favor of abortion is that unborn babies are not human persons because they lack certain features or activities. In an online article, "Personhood: Is a Fetus a Human Being?" **o** Joyce Arthur repeats some of the most common arguments when she claims that fetuses are not persons. We will list Arthur's points below, and then show the problems with her logic. Use the blank lines on this page to list more of your own thoughts.

They're too small.

Response: Exactly what size must we be in order to qualify as a person? All persons start out very small, whether it's the student sitting next to you in class, or the President of the United States. Some are considered "small" even when they grow into adults. Others get really big. If there's such a thing as being too small to be a person, is there such a thing as being too big? *Why would we want to exclude someone from personhood because of how big or small he is?*

They're not the right shape, and they lack a skeleton and internal organs.

Response: So what shape do we have to be to qualify as persons? Does it include having two arms and two legs? What about people who don't have any arms or legs? Are they not persons?

Some people have no feet. Some are born without eyes or ears or a nose. Some people lack certain internal organs their entire lives. Some people have no jaw, no hair, or no discernible neck. Many people are missing various bones in their skeletons. But we would never argue that these people are only partly human.

A one-celled human zygote, from the very beginning, has a unique and full human genome that is different from her mother's and father's. A fetus has a beating heart 18 days after conception, and at 21 days the heart is pumping blood through a closed circulatory system with a blood type that can be different from the mother's. At six weeks she has brainwaves.

At eight weeks, all of her body systems are present, and at eleven weeks they are all functioning.

Of course someone could argue that at earlier stages the embryo lacks these things. But that is because she does not need them yet to survive. As we will see, the potential for every organ is present from day one. *So why would we want to exclude someone from personhood because of her shape or the number of internal organs she has? If she can survive without them, why should she be disqualified from personhood?*

In the early stages they look like fish or aliens, and in later stages they look the same as dog and pig fetuses.

Response: There are actually a number of differences in the physical appearance of dog, pig, and human fetuses. But regardless, the way that human beings look during their early development has nothing to do with the definition of a human person. Appearances are a very incomplete way to define anything. Many adult people look like their dogs (or their dogs look like them). Does that make them dogs, or their dogs human? *Why would we want to exclude someone from personhood because of his physical appearance?*

At the very beginning of their existence, you can't see them with your naked eye.

Response: What difference does it make whether or not we can see someone with the naked eye? We can't see astronauts in outer space with the naked eye either, but they are still persons. There are lots of things we can't see without assistance — the rings of Saturn, bacteria, atoms. Our inability to see a tiny human zygote without the aid of a microscope does not make him any less human, or any less an individual. *Why would we want to exclude someone from personhood because we can't see him?*

They can't breathe, make sounds, or see.

Response: Why does someone have to breathe, make sounds, or see in order to qualify as a person? Although the fetus does not breathe the way that most born people do, he does exchange oxygen and carbon dioxide through the placenta, and makes breathing motions to help develop his lungs. If we must breathe a certain way in order to qualify as a person, what about people who need help breathing through oxygen tanks, tracheal tubes, or ventilators?

Of course, someone could make the claim that in the early stages the embryo doesn't breathe at all. This is true. But that's because the embryo doesn't need to breathe to survive. So why should she be disqualified?

Furthermore, cows and sheep breathe too, but they are not human

WHY WOULD YOU EXCLUDE SOMEONE FROM PERSONHOOD FOR ANY OF THESE REASONS?

Google "people who look like their pets" and see what you get.

persons. There are actually people who can hold their breath for up to 18 minutes. Are they not persons during the time that they are not breathing?

The same thing is true with the argument about making sounds or being able to see. Babies can see, taste, feel, smell, and hear in the womb between three and four months of development. And they would be able to make all sorts of audible sounds if it weren't for the fact that they are surrounded by amniotic fluid. In any case, what difference does any of this make? If you hold your breath, make no sounds, and close your eyes, are you no longer a person? What about blind people or mute people? *Why would we want to exclude someone from personhood for any of these reasons?*

DID YOU KNOW THAT BABIES HAVE MEMORY AS EARLY AS 30 WEEKS IN THE WOMB?

They eat through an umbilical cord, and not through a mouth.

Response: What difference does it make how we eat? Turtles and fish eat through their mouths, but they are not persons. People in hospitals must often eat through intravenous tubes. Is their personhood suspended during that time? *Why would we want to exclude someone from personhood because of how she eats?*

Their brains are not capable of conscious thought or memory.

Response: Actually, the brain starts functioning at six weeks after fertilization, and recent studies are showing that babies have memory as early as 30 weeks in the womb. Scientists believe that the human brain does not reach it's highest stage of development until 22 or 23 years old. And only a few short years after that, people begin gradually losing brain function.

Furthermore, people who are unconscious are not capable of conscious thought, and many people of different ages lose their ability to remember. So we can conclude that the stage of brain development has nothing to do with whether or not someone is a human person. *Why would we want to exclude someone from personhood just because they are not, at the moment, engaging in conscious thought or memory?*

They don't participate in society and are not recognized members of society.

Response: People who are in solitary confinement, lost in the mountains, cast away at sea, watching television in their basements, or sleeping in their beds do not participate in society either. Some people *choose* not to participate in society, such as hermits who live in isolated places, or people who are recluses. Other people are too ill to participate. At certain points in history, Black people and women were not recognized members of society. *Why would we want to exclude someone from personhood on any of these grounds?*

They don't have a name or a social identity.

Response: How does giving someone a name magically make him or her into a person? Would that mean that people who have several names have greater personhood than people who have only one name? If you change your name, are you a different type of being? If you give your parrot a name, does he suddenly become a human person? If someone steals your social identity (say, by stealing your Social Security number), did he steal your personhood? *Why would we want to exclude someone from personhood just because he doesn't have a name?*

People don't value them as much.

Response: An argument could be made that this is partly because the abortion business has done so much to publicly dehumanize the unborn. On the other hand, according to most polls, at least 50% of the population *does* value unborn human beings as much as they value born human beings. Many men and women experience tremendous grief at the loss of an unborn child. Some people don't value the elderly or the disabled, but they are still persons. If people stop valuing gold, it's still gold. *Why would we want to exclude someone from personhood because of another person's inability to appreciate her value?*

A lot of them die before they are born.

Response: A lot of people die *after* they are born, too. Come to think of it, we all do. *Why would we want to exclude someone from personhood because members of her group sometimes die?*

Members of certain tribes frequently kill even their newborn babies.

Response: The way some people treat their children has nothing to do with whether or not those children are human beings. Some parents abuse their children. *Why should the reprehensible actions of some parents reduce the status of their children to subhuman?*

They have undeveloped abilities and potential.

Response: So do teenagers. So do adults. So do many old people. None of us ever completely finish developing our abilities and potential. There is always more that we could be achieving. *Why would we exclude someone from personhood just because they are not yet fully developed?*

Remember the principle of complete explanation: the best explanation accounts for the most data. And recall that to create a complete definition, describing physical attributes is just the first of four steps. Any theory of human personhood which treats persons as though they were just physical things with physical qualities is leaving out significant data.

In Chapter 3, we identified a complete, objective, and coherent definition of the human person: **a living being which contains a real and existing power to direct its own development toward fulfillment**

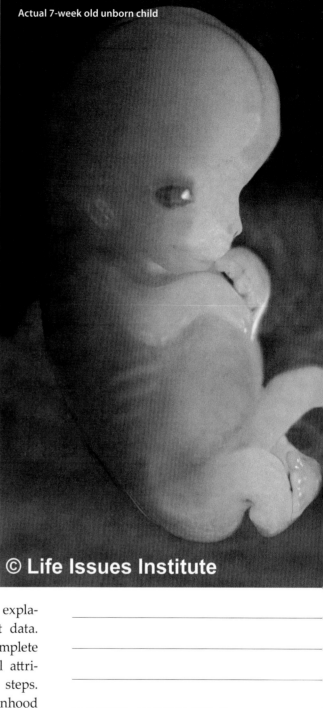

Got Questions? Write them here, and then use code **PCS246** to read frequently asked questions and answers. Or submit your own questions, and get answers!

© yuhirao / iStockphoto

through perfect, unconditional, and infinite Truth, Love, Goodness, Beauty, and Unity, and will do so if all the proper conditions are met.

Once someone tries to force a particular *physical* attribute into the definition of a human person (like having eyes, or immediately being able to talk or think), the definition will be **arbitrary**, because it will ignore the fact that the power to seek fulfillment through the transcendentals can exist even if someone has no eyes, isn't able to talk, and cannot yet form conscious thought.

Arbitrary means based on individual or subjective feelings or judgments, rather than based on reason and objective principles.

Whenever that power is present, there is human personhood that is worth protecting, regardless of whether the power is actually in use, or the power is just a potential that has yet to be actualized.

So according to the principle of complete explanation, an unborn baby, even from the moment of fertilization, must be considered a human person. Why? Because at the moment of fertilization, this new and unique individual has the power to direct its own development in the way that human persons develop. Nothing else needs to be added for the fertilized egg to begin developing as human beings do, except nourishment and time.

ABORTION AND THE PRINCIPLE OF OBJECTIVE EVIDENCE

For a claim to be reasonable, you must provide evidence that can be verified by others.

Recall that another way of stating this principle is, "arbitrarily asserted, arbitrarily denied." In the debate on page 42, Robert violates the principle of objective evidence by arbitrarily asserting that the fetus is not a human person. Emma violates the principle by arbitrarily asserting that it is. Neither one of them has any verifiable evidence. They only state their subjective beliefs. But there is objective and verifiable evidence that the unborn child, even from the moment of fertilization, *is* a human person.

Dr. Jerome Lejeune was a French geneticist who became famous in 1958 when he discovered the Trisomy 21 genetic condition responsible for causing Down Syndrome.

In the early 90s, Dr. Lejeune was called to testify in two abortion-related court cases.[P] He showed that a single-celled zygote, even before it implants in the mother's womb, has a full human genome, and proved that the genetic combination from both the mother and the father made the human zygote a very different being from her parents. In other words, the zygote is not like a hair cell or a skin cell. She's a unique individual. Finally, Dr. Lejeune showed that, under normal conditions, the genetic code present in the single-celled zygote was enough to guide the development of this individual into a fully actualized human adult.

All of this was proved using a scientific instrument called a DNA sequencer — which provided **empirical**, objective, and publicly verifiable evidence that the zygote is a unique, individual human being.

Let's suppose that some skeptics did not trust Dr. Lejeune's testimony. In that case, they could use his DNA sequencer and would end up with the same results. If they did not trust his machine, they could create their own DNA sequencer, and would still end up with the same results.

One argument made against Dr. Lejeune's testimony is that, although the full human genome may be present, it isn't fully actualized yet. In other words, the genome contains a lot of information, but it isn't being used to its fullest potential yet. This argument claims that we aren't *full* human persons until we have reached our *fullest* potential.

Even from a strictly biological point of view, this argument has serious problems. The full development of the brain, bone, tissue, and muscular systems doesn't occur until a person is 22 or 23 years old. Interestingly, shortly after reaching that age, we start to *lose* function. So if we have to be fully actualized biologically in order to be considered a full human being, the vast majority of people walking on

> THE GENETIC CODE IN A SINGLE-CELLED ZYGOTE DIRECTS THE SMALL PERSON TOWARD A BIOLOGICALLY COMPLETE ADULT.

the planet would be immediately disqualified. In fact, we wouldn't really know who qualified and who didn't, because we can't pinpoint the precise moment when someone has reached full biological actualization, and when they begin losing function.

Unless we are going to be arbitrary and subjective, we have to conclude that when a full, individual human genome exists, a full human being exists. After all, it is the only objective and publicly verifiable biological evidence. And when a full human being exists, a full human person exists.

THE UNBORN CHILD IS A HUMAN PERSON FROM THE MOMENT OF FERTILIZATION.

Therefore, the unborn child from the moment of fertilization is a full human person. Remember, this is not a claim that the unborn child is fully *developed* as a human person. It means that the unborn child is a full human person with human powers.

But what if someone counters that you don't know for sure that *all* human powers are present at fertilization? Maybe only *some* powers are present, like the biological ones that direct the growth of the body, but the transcendental powers don't show up until a later point in time. The answer to this is found in the principle of non-maleficence, which will be discussed in detail in Book 3.

The principle of non-maleficence holds that in times of doubt, we must err on the side of presuming that human personhood is present until we can prove otherwise. If we do not follow this principle, we risk committing a serious harm. We risk **legitimizing** all circumstances where human beings might be abused, oppressed, enslaved, killed, or injured simply because someone was "not sure it was a human person." Therefore, unless we can prove otherwise, we must assume that at fertilization, the full human person is present with all of its transcendental powers.

To **"legitimize"** something means to sanction it. To give it the green light or the "thumbs up."

© csreed / iStockphoto

Use code **PCS247** to access study tools for this chapter.

CONCLUSION

In the 1973 *Roe v. Wade* case, the United States Supreme Court decided that unborn children are *not* human persons. Their decision was based on the fact that a group of randomly selected experts who were gathered to testify could not come to agreement. Rather than look at the objective and publicly verifiable evidence, the Justices concluded that disagreement between experts was enough to disqualify unborn human beings from personhood. This subjective and arbitrary decision was not only unreasonable, it was also irresponsible, as it opened the way for millions of abortions in the years that followed.

When slavery was still practiced in the United States, there were highly educated and reputable "experts" on both sides of that issue as well. But the mere fact that disagreement existed did not mean that Black human beings were not persons in the fullest sense.

Human personhood is not just a subjective value judgment. As we saw in Chapters 1, 2, and 3, we can discover the definition of the human person through observation. This chapter has offered objective, verifiable evidence that the unborn child is a human person from the moment of fertilization.

This has serious implications for how we should view abortion. If abortion kills a real, unique, individual human person, then it would be an enormous violation of the most basic human right — the right to life.

The next book in this series will explore three principles of ethics and three principles of justice, including the principle of inalienable rights. Those six principles will provide further assistance in forming a sound position on abortion and other social issues.

Appendix

TEN UNIVERSAL PRINCIPLES OF CIVILIZATION

Principle of Identity and Values
(In Book One: *Identity & Values*)

1. **Principle of Beneficence (The Golden Rule)** "Do unto others as you would have them do unto you." (Do the good.)

Principles of Reason
(In Book Two: *Truth & Reason*)

2. **Principle of Non-Contradiction** "Something cannot be both X and not-X in the same respect at the same place and time."

3. **Principle of Complete Explanation** "The best explanation is the one which accounts for the most data."

4. **Principle of Objective Evidence** "For a claim to be reasonable, you must provide evidence that can be verified by others."

Principles of Ethics
(In Book Three: *Ethics & Justice*)

5. **Principle of Non-Maleficence (The Silver Rule)** "Do not do unto others what you would not have them do unto you." (Do no harm.)

6. **Principle of Consistent Ends and Means** "The ends do not justify the means." (You cannot use an evil method to achieve a good result.)

7. **Principle of Full Human Potential** "Every human being deserves to be valued according to what he is capable of achieving at his highest potential; not according to the development he has achieved at a particular time."

Principles of Justice
(Also in Book Three: *Ethics & Justice*)

8. **Principle of Natural Rights** "All human beings in themselves (because of their existence alone) have the inalienable right to life, liberty, and property ownership. No government gives these rights, and no government can take them away."

9. **Principle of the Hierarchy of Rights** "Any right which is a necessary condition for the very possibility of another right's existence is the more fundamental right. In a conflict of rights, the more fundamental right should take priority."

10. **Principle of Limits to Freedom** "Creating a new right for some people is wrong if it becomes a burdensome duty for others." (One person's right cannot become another person's duty to die, suffer, or be unfairly burdened.)

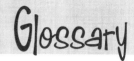

Glossary

agape **love:** selfless love that recognizes the unique preciousness of each and every human being.

arbitrary: based on individual or subjective feelings or judgments, rather than based on reason and objective principles.

beneficence: to do good for others.

common understanding: thinking that is shared in common with most other people. When most reasonable people in most places in most time periods throughout history share the same understanding about what is good and what is evil, there is a strong probability that what is being understood is true.

conscience: the ability of our reason (our intellect) to judge, here and now, whether a particular act that we are about to do, or are in the process of doing, or have done already, is good or evil. A well-formed conscience approves what is good and rejects what is evil. It is like a sixth sense of knowing when something is right or wrong.

empirical: able to be known through the five senses; known through observation and experience rather than through logic.

essence: the intrinsic nature of a thing; what a thing is at its very heart and core.

ethical relativism: sometimes called "moral relativism" or "situation ethics," it is the position that there is no real standard for determining right or wrong conduct.

ethics: a set of standards by which a community judges the rightness or wrongness of human actions.

factual truth: truth which can be verified through the five senses.

first principle: a principle which is necessary to accept before you can prove or disprove anything. First principles are so basic that they do not need to be proved by other proofs. They prove themselves. Example: A = A.

inferior: to be lower in quality or value.

legitimize: to sanction or to give something the "green light" or a "thumbs up."

maleficence: to do evil or harm to someone else.

marginalized: to be pushed off to the side and not given the same rights and protections as the rest of society. Minorities, refugees, elderly persons, dying persons, and unborn human beings are examples of frequently marginalized people.

morality: the goodness or evilness of human actions.

nominal definition: assigns a name to a thing. Nominal definitions are the basis of language, without which we could not communicate.

objective ethics: holds that goodness is an actual reality that exists in itself. It is not just a theory or a principle, but a real, existing entity. Objective ethics holds that there is objective moral truth, and it exists for everybody, in every place, and in every time. It is the position that there are objective standards for judging human acts.

objective evidence: evidence that can be verified by anyone who is able to use their five senses, or by anyone who is intelligent enough to follow an argument.

objective truth: a state of reality that is true in and of itself, regardless of anyone's opinions or perceptions, and regardless of the place or time that the reality is being observed. It is not affected by the personal feelings or biases of the people observing it. Objective truth is also sometimes called "absolute truth."

philosophy: literally, "love of wisdom" — from the Greek words *philo* (meaning "love") and *sophia* (meaning "wisdom"). Aristotle defined philosophy as "the knowledge of being" — or the study of what is true about human existence versus what is not true.

principle: a basic or fundamental truth that is used to support a line of reasoning, a belief, or a way of behaving.

principles of reason: principles that help us to logically arrive at what is true.

real definition: a complete definition that tries to get at the essence of what you are describing; not imposed arbitrarily, but observed and discovered from the intrinsic nature of the thing being defined.

reason: the ability of the human mind to think things through logically.

Glossary

relativism: the theory that truth is relative or subjective, differing according to events or persons. Relativism claims that "what's true for me is true for me, and what's true for you is true for you," and argues that all points of view are equally valid.

revelation: God's self disclosure; God communicating Himself and His divine plan to us through events, persons, and, Christians believe, most fully in Jesus Christ.

self-evident truth: something that is objectively true in and of itself, and is true for all times, places, and persons.

social ethical issue: an ethical issue caused by the actions (or failure to act) of people or societies; includes issues like world hunger, war, prejudice, international poverty, and the oppression of marginalized people.

subjective evidence: evidence that can be verified only by the individual having the experience.

subjective truth: a state of reality that can change depending on who is perceiving it, or where or when it is being perceived.

subordinate: to be under the power or authority of someone else.

telos: the Greek word for "end," "final goal," or "full purpose"; the point at which a thing reaches its fullest stage of development — the fullest form of its power; similar to *"to ti en einai"* which means, "what it was to be" or "what it was meant to be."

transcend: to rise above or go beyond the limits of the physical or material world.

transcendental: a reality that goes beyond physical reality.

truth: whatever corresponds with what is real. Aristotle clarified: "To say of what *is* that it *is*, and of what *is not* that it *is not*, is true."

universal: relating to every person, in every place, at every time.

Endnotes

A "All Things Considered." National Public Radio. May 2, 2005

B Aristotle, *Metaphysics* 1011b25

C *Bahá'u'lláh*, Gleanings, LXVI:8

D *Udanavarga* 5:18

E Matthew 7:1

F *Analects* XV.24 (trans. by David Hinton)

G Brihaspati, Mahabharata Book 13 (Anusasana Parva, Section CXIII, Verse 8)

H Kitab al-Kafi, vol. 2, p. 146

I Talmud, *Shabbat* 31a, the "Great Principle"

J Aristotle, *Metaphysics*, 1006a15. See also 1006a30-1008a10

K See, for example, "This Thing Called Love" by Laren Slater (*National Geographic*, February 2006, pp. 32-49)

L Peter Singer, FAQ. http://www.princeton.edu/~psinger/faq.html. Accessed July 12, 2012

M Peter Singer, FAQ. http://www.princeton.edu/~psinger/faq.html. Accessed July 12, 2012

N *Dred Scott v. Sandford*, 60 U.S. 393, 1857. This court case is sometimes dated 1856. This discrepancy is because 1856 is the year that the court heard the case. But the decision was rendered and read in March of 1857

O Joyce Arthur. "Personhood: Is a Fetus a Human Being?" 2001. http://www.abortionaccess.info/fetusperson.htm. Accessed July 12, 2012

P *New Jersey v. Alexander Loce* (1991), and *Davis v. Davis*, 842 S.W.2d 588, 597 (1992)

Index

A

abortion
   Principle of Complete
      Explanation and, 44-48
   Principle of Non-Contradiction
      and, 42-43
   Principle of Objective Evidence
      and, 49-50
   agape, 35, 41
alternate reality, 7
arbitrary
   definition of, 19, 25
   definition of persons, 41, 48, 50
Aristotle,
   definitions and, 29-30
   essence and, 29
   first principles and, 7-8
   material cause, 30
   philosopher, 1
   philosophy and, 1
   physical description and, 30
   Principle of Non-Contradiction
      and, 22
   telos and, 32
   truth and, 2

B

Baha'i, 10
beneficence, see also Golden Rule,
      18, 20-21
Buddhism, 10

C

Christianity, 9, 10
common understanding, 10
complete explanation, see also
      Principle of Complete
      Explanation
   abortion and, 44-48
   application to social issues, 39-40
   Aristotle and, 29
   definition of, 20, 23-24

defining a human person
      and, 35-38
   definitions and, 30
   Principles of Reason and, 21
conditions, 29
Confucianism, 10
conscience, 12-14
consistent ends and means, 18

D

divine revelation, 14, 15
DNA, 34-35, 49
Down Syndrome, 49
Dred Scott, 28, 40-41

E

empirical, 35, 49
essence, 29
ethical relativism, 9
ethics, 9
   objective ethics, 9

F

factual truth, 3-4, 7
fetus, 15, 42-45, 49
final cause, 29
first principle(s)
   Aristotle and, 7-8
full human potential, 18
full purpose, 29

G

Golden Rule, see also Principle of
      Beneficence and Silver Rule
   definition and, 21
   love and, 15

H

hierarchy of rights, 18
Hinduism, 10
human being
   definition of, 27-28
   defining a, 33-38
   racism and, 41
   unborn and, 43-51
human person
   abortion and, 42-51
   defining a, 27, 33-38, 41

I

inferior, 41
Islam, 10

J

Jesus, 15
Judaism, 10

L

Laci and Conner's Law, 43
legitimize, 50
Lejeune, Dr. Jerome, 49
limits to freedom 18

M

maleficence, 18, 50
marginalized, 19-20
material cause, 30
moral relativism, 9
morality, 9

Index

N

natural rights, 18

nominal definition, 29, 33

non-contradiction
    abortion and, 42-43
    Aristotle and, 22
    defining the human person
        and, 37
    definition of, 22-22
    Principles of Reason and, 21

non-maleficence, see also Silver
        Rule, 18, 50

O

objective ethics, 9

objective evidence
    abortion and, 49-50
    application to social issues, 39-40
    defining the human person
        and, 34
    definition of, 24-25
    Principles of Reason and, 21

objective truth, 3-6, 9, 20, 24

P

person
    abortion and, 42-50
    definition of, 9, 27-28, 33-38
    Dred Scott, 28, 40-41
    Roe v. Wade, 41-42, 51

philia, 1

philosophy, 1

physical description, 30, 31, 34

powers, 29

principle
    definition of, 8, 18
    Ten Universal Principles, 18-25

Principle of Beneficence, see also
        Golden Rule, 18, 20-21

Principle of Complete Explanation
    abortion and, 44-48
    application to social issues, 39-40

Aristotle and, 29
definition of, 20, 23-24
defining a human person
    and, 35-38
definitions and, 30
Principles of Reason and, 21

**Principle of Consistent Ends and
    Means,** 18

Principle of Full Human Potential,
    18

**Principle of the Hierarchy of
    Rights,** 18

Principle of Limits to Freedom, 18
    Principle of Natural Rights, 18
    Principle of Non-Contradiction
    abortion and, 42-43
    Aristotle and, 22
    defining the human person
        and, 37
    definition of, 22-22
    Principles of Reason and, 21

Principle of Non-Maleficence,
        see also Silver Rule, 18, 50

Principle of Objective Evidence
    abortion and, 49-50
    application to social issues, 39-40
    defining the human person
        and, 34
    definition of, 24-25
    Principles of Reason and, 21

Principles of Reason, 17-25

R

real definition, 29-30, 34

reason
    definition of, 10-11
    principles of, 17-25

relativism
    definition of, 4
    ethical relativism, 9
    truth and, 9

revelation, 14, 15

Roe v. Wade, 41-42, 51

S

self-evident, 3-4, 8, 25

Silver Rule
    definition of, 10
    faiths and, 10
    Golden Rule, 21
    Principle of Non-Maleficence, 18,
    50

situation ethics, 9

slavery, 10-11, 28, 51

social ethical issue, 19-20

sophia, 1

soul, 35-36, 41

subjective evidence, 25

subjective truth, 3

subordinate, 41

Supreme Court, U.S.
    Dred Scott, 28, 40-41
    Roe v. Wade, 41-42, 51
    telos, 32, 36

T

Ten Universal Principles, 18-25

transcend, 35, 41

transcendental, 5, 41, 48, 50

truth
    Aristotle and, 2
    relativism and, 9

U

**Unborn Victims of Violence
    Act of 2004,** 43

universal
    definition of, 18
    truth, 3, 5
    Ten Universal Principles, 18-19

Z

zygote, 44-45, 49